Parliaments and Legislatures
Janet M. Box-Steffensmeier and David T. Canon, Series Editors

Doing the Right Thing

*Collective Action and Procedural Choice
in the New Legislative Process*

LAWRENCE BECKER

The Ohio State University Pres
Columbus

Library of Congress Cataloging-in-Publication Data

Becker, Lawrence, 1969–
    Doing the right thing : collective action and procedural choice in the new
legislative process / Lawrence Becker.
        p. cm. — (Parliaments and legislatures)
    Includes bibliographical references and index.
    ISBN 0-8142-0985-8 (cloth : alk. paper) — ISBN 0-8142-9059-0 (CD-ROM)
    1. Legislation—United States—History. 2. United States. Congress—
Rules and practice—History. 3. Parliamentary practice—United States—
Case studies. 4. Legislation—United States—Case studies. I. Title. II. Series.
    KF4945.B43 2005
    328.73—dc22
                                                        2004019796
Paper (ISBN: 978-0-8142-5611-4)
Cover design by Dan O'Dair
Type set in Sabon

CONTENTS

LIST OF TABLES

PREFACE AND ACKNOWLEDGMENTS

It is no wonder the American Congress is among the most reviled of American institutions, political or otherwise. We know a great deal about the institution, its structure and constitutional power, its organization, and the people who inhabit it and their behavior. Unfortunately, much of what we pass on to students is quite negative in tone. The institution is frequently depicted as gridlocked, impotent, overly influenced by special interests, and even corrupt. Political scientists would seem to be at least partly to blame for this impression. Far from disputing these notions, our models of legislative organization and behavior appear to confirm them by utilizing the electoral motivation as an organizing principle and treating legislators as utility maximizers interested in accruing "gains from trade."

While there is a great deal to be learned from these models and from these organizing principles, this book is animated by the welcome observation that Congress does sometimes do the right thing. The "right" thing is an admittedly subjective concept; but meeting the literature on Congress on its own terms, we might argue that Congress is doing the "right" thing when it enacts policies that confer benefits widely perceived to be in the public interest while imposing costs on small, concentrated, and, as a result, powerful groups. By this definition, Congress does the "right" thing far more often than the bulk of the literature would have us believe. I do not wade into the difficult question of why they do this; rather this book is completely focused on the question of *how* members of Congress do the right thing. As we will come to see, the deft manipulation of procedures is a critical component of doing the right thing. These procedural maneuvers remain a remarkably underappreciated and misunderstood part of the legislative process. They are underappreciated in a scholarly literature that does not recognize the central role they can play in altering policy outcomes. They are misunderstood in a scholarly literature that too frequently portrays them as tools designed to frustrate accountability and responsibility by members of the contemporary Congress. In this book, I seek to add some balance to that portrayal of America's central lawmaking institution.

This project could never have been completed without the kindness, patience, support, and guidance of a wide variety of people. My dissertation advisor, John Hird, offered helpful comments and a guiding hand throughout the process and he was very generous with his most precious resource—his time. He always read drafts of chapters faster than I could celebrate their completion and provided constructive advice in coping with the most difficult theoretical problems I encountered. This study is far more coherent and interesting for his efforts, and what problems remain are my responsibility alone. I would also like to thank the members of my dissertation committee, Fred Kramer and Ralph Whitehead. They agreed to serve on my committee despite a host of other commitments when I had no reward to give other than my thanks, and they offered useful suggestions along the way. I appreciate their sacrifice of time and energy, and I hope the final product can serve as a partial payment of the debt I owe to them.

A number of other scholars provided important feedback, insight, and assistance for which I am thankful. Vin Moscardelli and Craig Thomas helped me more than they know both in casual discussions of the literature in their fields and by suggesting new ideas and directions for my research. Their encouragement kept me going and their intelligence made this project far better than it otherwise would have been. Jessica Korn inspired my interest in congressional procedures, read drafts of my chapters along the way, and always asked the tough questions that made the focus of this project more clear. She has been both my toughest critic and a caring friend and I thank her for serving in both roles. Jerry Mileur and George Sulzner deserve special thanks for all they have done for me. I learned much of what I know about politics from them and I learned even more from them about how to be a good person. For their kindness, generosity, encouragement, and good cheer, I owe them a debt I can never repay. I also owe a debt of gratitude to my colleagues at California State University, Northridge. The institution has supported and encouraged my research in ways that exceeded my expectations; my various colleagues have served a variety of roles, including mentor, friend, and everything in between.

I could never have completed this project without the support of my family. My parents, my step-parents, each of my brothers, and my Aunt Helen and Uncle Werner offered me encouragement, financial support, and a variety of safe havens away from academia when I needed them most. My nieces and nephew, Brooke, Ethan, and Alaina offered the most priceless gift of all—relaxation and escape in their sweet smiles.

My friends kept me going by offering encouragement, caring, good times, and cheer even when I proved a reluctant receiver of their gifts. Wendy Abels, Ezra and Michele Angrist, Todd Audyatis, Amy and Max Dowling, Nick Dungey, Jerold and Kara Duquette, Peter Fairman, Lisa and Mike Hannahan,

Tom Hogen-Esch, Ahmed Idris, Ingrid Jaeger, Eric Katz, Jon Keller, Bob Lacey, Doug Lathrop, Genia Onokhin, Mike Reese, Stan Rosenberg, Martin Saiz, Julia and Lonce Sandy-Bailey, Matt Schmill, Angie Schock, Adam Shrager, Jeff and Kate Schwartz, Jennie Stump, and Jeanne Zaino should all know this would never have been completed without them.

Finally, Jennie deForest has been an unending source of strength, good counsel, and happiness at every difficult stage for me. This quick mention of her importance to me cannot do justice to my appreciation for everything she does in my behalf. It is a measure of her character that she wouldn't even expect to be mentioned here and that self-confident modesty is just one of the reasons she owns my heart.

ONE

Introduction

During the late 1980s and early 1990s, the United States Congress was finally able to put into place a procedure that closed a significant number of military installations around the country, both improving the force posture of the American military and saving billions of precious dollars for the general treasury. What makes the case of military base closure so interesting to students of American government is not the novelty of the idea—most military policy analysts had been arguing for many years that the United States had too many military installations—but rather, the fact that the Congress was able to do it. Cases, like military base closure, where Congress "did the right thing,"[1] were not all that infrequent during the 1980s and 1990s; however, political scientists had a tendency during this same time period to treat these cases more as one-of-a-kind freakish accidents than anything else.

The fact is that political scientists have always had an easy time explaining the passage of particularistic legislation—legislation that confers benefits on localities or particular economic sectors at the expense of the entire nation such as local construction projects or subsidies for particular industries. What political scientists have not had such an easy time explaining, however, is legislation that does the opposite—legislation that imposes direct costs on localities or particular economic sectors in favor of some general, diffuse benefit such as deficit reduction. Despite this difficulty, many examples of this type of legislation exist: military bases have been closed; special interest tax loopholes have been eliminated in favor of general tax rate reduction; targeted tax increases and spending cuts have been approved, affecting a variety of programs and regions in favor of deficit reduction; national nuclear waste sites have been chosen; and NAFTA was adopted despite the fact that it was an agreement that ended a number of subsidies and regulations protecting particular industries in favor of the general goal of promoting free trade.

In *The Logic of Congressional Action*, R. Douglas Arnold (1990, 5) works to fill this gap in the literature by developing a theory of congressional

1

policymaking that "allows for the triumph of any one of three competing interests—general, group, or geographic." Arnold argues there are generally three types of strategies—strategies of persuasion, procedural strategies, and strategies of modification—available to those attempting to build winning coalitions in the legislative process. But significantly, he points out (Arnold 1990, 116) that it is procedural strategies that "are most attractive when legislators decide to impose costs on either attentive or inattentive publics." Procedural strategies are designed to alter the political calculus confronting individual legislators on particular votes by either strengthening or weakening the causal chain between legislator action and policy effects. Thus, by utilizing procedural strategies such as a closed rule, omnibus legislation, writing legislation in secrecy, or delegating decisions to an agency, individual members of Congress can free themselves from more parochial concerns and can vote to support general, late-order benefits while imposing particularistic, early-order costs on attentive publics.[2] Indeed, in her well-received book, *Unorthodox Lawmaking: New Legislative Processes in the U.S. Congress*, Barbara Sinclair points out that the use of these special types of procedures has become so widespread in the passage of major legislation that our textbook understanding of how a bill becomes a law is now dated. She adds, "no single model has replaced it. Variety, not uniformity, characterizes the contemporary legislative process" (Sinclair 2000, 218).

What Sinclair does not address in her detailed account of the use of "unorthodox" procedures in the legislative process, however, is the increasing use of what I call "extra-congressional" legislative procedures. If what had previously been considered unorthodox—closed rules, the use of omnibus legislative vehicles, post-committee adjustments to legislation, the avoidance of committees altogether in legislating, and legislating in conference—has become the new orthodoxy, the new unorthodox procedures may be those that formally delegate the power to craft policy alternatives to institutions other than Congress.[3]

Defining Extra-Congressional Legislative Procedures

Extra-congressional legislative procedures are *those adopted by Congress that grant formal power to craft the specifics of particularistic costs to ad hoc institutions outside of Congress and, in some cases, to impose those costs without explicit congressional approval.* Examples of these extra-congressional procedures include the base-closure procedures of the late 1980s and early 1990s, the Gramm-Rudman-Hollings deficit-control procedure, the recent line-item veto procedure, and fast-track trade agreement approval procedures.

These procedures all have several characteristics in common. First, each is an ad hoc response to congressional difficulty in dealing with a particular policy problem at a particular moment in time. The Gramm-Rudman-Hollings procedure, for instance, was designed to reach specific deficit targets in specific years. Fast-track procedures utilized in the passage of NAFTA were designed and approved for this particular trade negotiation and no other. The line-item veto procedure, which granted enhanced rescission authority to the president (and thus allowed the president to cancel spcific spending items or tax breaks), could be used only on appropriations and a very limited number of tax provisions and, more importantly, was granted only for a certain number of years. It was created to deal with the problem of pork-barrel legislation in the late 1990s. Given the tension President Clinton's rescissions created and the fact that the Supreme Court struck down the mechanism as violating the separation of powers, it is highly unlikely the enhanced rescission authority will be renewed anytime soon. Finally, the base-closure procedures were authorized only for specific rounds of base closures in 1988, 1991, 1993, and 1995. Significantly, unlike when Congress creates an agency, a new law, or even a new rule to guide deliberations in one of its chambers, these procedures all contain some temporal limitation.[4] Not one of these procedures remains in use today despite the fact that each was adopted within the last twenty years.

Second, these extra-congressional legislative procedures all grant formal authority to design a package of particularistic cuts to an institution outside Congress, whether it be a bipartisan commission, the president, an agency, or a particular agency official. For example, Congress delegated power to the Defense Base Closure and Realignment Commission to draw up a list of bases to be closed or realigned and empowered the Pentagon and the president to implement the recommendations unless Congress passed a joint resolution to disapprove the list. A wide variety of authors have made the mistake of lumping the base closure commission into the same category as other commissions such as the Greenspan Commission on Social Security in the early 1980s.[5] Indeed, commissions and task forces have been utilized throughout the twentieth century for a variety of purposes. One characteristic that distinguishes the Defense Base Closure and Realignment Commission from the rest, however, is its statutory authority to frame and implement a particular policy alternative. While Greenspan's commission had informal political clout, it did not have the formal power to implement its recommendations or even to force Congress or the president to consider its recommendations.

Each of these procedures involved some kind of formal delegation of authority similar to the base-closure commission. The line-item veto gave the president formal authority to cancel individual appropriations. Fast-track procedures provided formal power to the president to negotiate a trade agreement that Congress would be obliged to consider without amendments. The Gramm-Rudman-Hollings law delegated formal power to the Office of Management and Budget (OMB) to impose automatic cuts in most government programs and agencies if deficit targets were not met.

Finally, each of these extra-congressional procedures is designed to provide at least the appearance of legislators being kept at an arm's length distance from the creation of the final policy product while still at least allowing legislators the option to disapprove the chosen policy alternative.[6] Legislators could stop Gramm-Rudman-Hollings sequesters from taking effect, they could stop the base closure list in toto, they could stop NAFTA from being implemented, and they could override the president's decision to rescind funds, but they could not alter the substance of these policies at the margins.

Perhaps more importantly, when any of these policy alternatives were enacted, no single legislator could be held accountable as the author of a particular policy effect. It was the base-closure commission that drew up the list of bases to be closed, and the procedure even afforded individual legislators an opportunity to go on the record opposing the list. It was the entire Congress that would presumably miss a deficit target under the Gramm-Rudman-Hollings law and it was OMB that would initiate the automatic spending cuts. It was the president who was responsible for line-item veto cuts and the particular provisions of NAFTA. In short, individual legislators were provided extraordinary causal distance from the negative policy effects of particularistic pain.

Extra-Congressional Legislative Procedures and the Legislative Process

Though Arnold does suggest that procedural strategies are preferable in cases where coalition leaders seek to make cuts in particularistic benefits in favor of some general benefit, he provides little in the way of guidance on how coalition leaders choose between alternative procedural strategies. These extra-congressional procedures are still the exception rather than the rule. Nevertheless, there are enough examples of their use (and they are being utilized to address sufficiently similar policy problems) that it has become important to ask why, in some cases, Congress uses the internal congressional procedures Sinclair considers to be the new orthodoxy and why, in other cases, Congress uses these extra-congressional procedures.[7]

This poses the central avenue of inquiry for this book. Why, for instance, did legislators employ extra-congressional procedures in the case of base closure and use the regular internal procedures of Congress to shepherd tax reform through the legislature in 1986? It is simply not plausible to assert that coalition leaders attempting to close military bases thought of the idea of a commission to shield legislators from the political pain and coalition leaders attempting to cut special interest tax loopholes did not. These two groups of coalition leaders *chose* their particular procedural mechanisms for a reason or some set of reasons.

Toward a Theory of Procedural Choice

A variety of existing theories on legislative organization, legislative behavior, and legislative delegation lead us to a number of propositions about procedural choice that we will explore in the case studies in the following chapters. While none of these propositions is in itself determinative, when taken together they do constitute what we might consider to be a comprehensive theory of procedural choice. A couple of notes of caution are in order here. First, while I do intend to suggest that this theory of procedural choice should be testable and generalizable, I also recognize the difficulty more empirically oriented social scientists may have "proving" the theory's merit. As we will see, each of the following five propositions is effectively based on gauging a particular case's place on a continuum that is not readily quantifiable. In this sense, the theory is more intended to shed light on the (sometimes diametrically opposed) forces pushing Congress toward a particular procedural avenue than it is to suggest a certain and quantifiable prediction about what Congress will do. Second, while the decision to delegate or not to delegate is often depicted in "all or nothing" terms, the truth is that there are many shades of gray in between total delegation and a total lack of delegation. It is inaccurate, therefore, to think about this project as seeking to explain "delegation or no delegation." Rather, I seek to explain the conditions under which legislators will seek to delegate more or less.

Proposition I. Geographic Concentration of Costs

In adopting policies that impose direct costs on specific groups in favor of some general benefit, does the type of group incurring the cost make any difference?

Is it easier to impose costs on one type of group than on another? Arnold (1990, 26) suggests two categories of particularism which he refers to as "group costs and benefits" and "geographic costs and benefits." Group costs and benefits are those incurred by a particular category of people who may be delineated by their age, income, occupation, industry, race, gender, or hobby. Geographic costs and benefits, Arnold goes on to tell us, are simply a special kind of group cost or benefit—one in which geographic location is the common element. While geographic and nongeographic groups are not mutually exclusive, Arnold (1990, 26) states,

> the distinction is nevertheless useful, both because geographic areas enjoy direct representation in Congress whereas other groups do not and because the recipients of geographic benefits (and the payers of geographic costs) are necessarily in close proximity to one another whereas their counterparts who receive group benefits (or pay group costs) may have absolutely no contact.

The distinction is apparently important. It finds its way into much of the literature on Congress.[8] Furthermore, while Arnold suggests that geographic benefits are more difficult to cut,[9] Kenneth R. Mayer (1995, 394) makes the point more explicitly, arguing that collective action problems are "particularly acute when the affected groups form geographic constituencies, rather than more dispersed economic or social interests." The "acute" nature of these geographically concentrated costs leads us to Proposition I.

Proposition I, Geographic Concentration—The more geographically concentrated the particularistic costs being imposed are, the more likely it is that Congress will delegate authority and employ some sort of extra-congressional legislative procedure.

Simply put, when legislators are seeking to confer some general benefit that will impose geographically concentrated costs, we will see that there is extraordinary pressure to avoid being connected in any way with those costs. In terms of procedural choice, this means legislators have an extraordinary incentive to employ an extra-congressional procedure of some kind. In examining the geographic concentration of particularistic costs in the chapters to come, we will find that, in many ways, this first proposition is also a "first among equals." While not determinative in itself, it is always a primary concern and, therefore, a key factor in procedural choice.

Proposition II. Scope of the Policy Area

Many mechanisms within the normal legislative process offer legislative leaders tools to obfuscate the link between individual legislators and the negative policy consequences of particularistic costs. As a result, the use of closed rules, omnibus legislative vehicles, and legislating in secrecy are not very unusual sights in Congress. But ultimately, all these procedural tactics require that some legislator, some committee, or some group of party leaders craft the final policy alternative. This means that some legislator, committee, or group of party leaders must be intimately connected with the direct costs that legislation imposes on concentrated (geographic or otherwise) groups. From this perspective then, one might wonder why Congress does not delegate in every situation of this sort. The reason, of course, is that delegation poses its own set of problems for legislators.

In their generalized theory of delegation, Kiewiet and McCubbins (1991) refer to one such problem as "Madison's dilemma"—a reference to the logic employed by James Madison in justifying the use of "auxiliary precautions" such as the separation of powers, bicameralism, and federalism as a counterbalance to "a dependence on the people" in American constitutionalism. On the one hand, the principal must delegate enough power to allow the agent to carry out his or her duties. But on the other, the principal must find some way of limiting the agent's power so that it is exercised as closely to the way the principal wants it exercised as possible. The fear is that delegating power will incur "agency losses"[10] that will outweigh the benefits of delegating in the first place. The point, for Kiewiet and McCubbins then, is that principals will delegate power only if the delegation includes some method of containing agency losses.

It is clear, however, that opportunities for containing agency losses are not the same across policy areas. Specifically, policy areas that are narrow are better candidates for delegation because the nature of the policy area serves as a natural limit on the agent's discretion.[11] In contrast, we would expect that the delegation of authority to impose particularistic costs is less likely in the case of broad policy areas because it would be more difficult to limit the jurisdiction of the agent in the way this can be done in more narrow policy areas.[12] Thus, one factor that we can examine in addition to geography is the scope of the policy area.

☙☙

Proposition II, Scope of the Policy Area—The more narrow the policy area in question, the more likely Congress is to delegate authority and employ some form of extra-congressional procedure.

While the preceding discussion focuses on blame avoidance[13] as a reason legislators might be more willing to delegate authority in narrow versus broad policy areas, there is also a positive reason reinforcing this blame avoidance. Just as narrow policy areas offer fewer opportunities for negative policy consequences in legislators' districts, they also offer fewer opportunities for noticeable policy benefits that accrue to the general public. The cases in question—cases in which Congress cuts particularistic benefits in favor of some general benefit—are difficult precisely because legislators fear that those who will benefit (the general public) will be unlikely to notice or appreciate the benefit while those who bear costs (groups and constituencies) will certainly notice and care. That stated, there is a difference between broad and narrow policy areas in the extent to which the general public will notice and appreciate the general benefit. Because some policy areas, like tax reform, are more broad than base closure, a vote for the general benefit of tax reform has more electoral value than a vote for the general benefits offered by base closure.

As a result, members of Congress have two reasons to delegate authority in narrow versus broad policy areas. In narrow policy areas, members are more likely to avoid the agency losses associated with delegation *and* they are also less able to credibly claim credit for helping to deliver a general benefit. For both blame-avoidance and credit-claiming reasons, then, the scope of the policy area becomes an important potential factor in determining when and why legislative leaders employ their own internal procedures and when and why they utilize extra-congressional procedures in cutting particularistic benefits in favor of some general benefit.

Proposition III. Political Time

Another factor that impacts procedural choice is suggested by Stephen Skowronek (2003), who argues that presidential leadership is constrained, in part, by its particular moment within an historical epoch. While Skowronek's study is focused on presidential power, this simple yet elegant concept can easily be extended to apply to other institutions.

But what does "political time" mean for procedural choice and what directional impact is it likely to have? Generally, there are three ways in which the moment in political time offers opportunities and constraints to coalition leaders seeking to impose particularistic costs while conferring general benefits. First, while I do not delve deeply into the question of what motivates legislative leaders to pursue the policy outcomes they do, it is clear that the particular kind of policy outcomes with which this study is concerned require some consensus or near consensus among elites, and sometimes among the public, that something needs to be done.[14] As we will see, in base closure, in tax reform, in nuclear waste, and in trade policy, the emergence of a near consensus among elites about the general direction of policy is a necessary precondition of action. The more widely held the consensus, the more likely it is that members of Congress will be willing to pursue an internal procedural strategy.

Second, coalition leaders seeking to enact the types of policies described here must be sensitive to the unique institutional developments in the policy area involved. For instance, if there has there been a history of mistrust between the Congress and the relevant agency involved in the policy area, the option of delegating authority to that agency may not be politically viable. Similarly, structural features *within* the Congress (committee power, party power, rules, norms, etc.) are not fixed over the long term. A pattern of mistrust with an outside agent will obviously make it less likely legislators will delegate authority. Additionally, the development of institutions within the Congress that allow members to shield themselves from negative electoral retribution will likely lead members to pursue an internal procedural strategy.

Finally, coalition leaders must be sensitive to the electoral calendar when enacting policies such as these. Votes in Congress, administrative decisions, and policy impacts can be timed to occur later or earlier, before or after an election, or at the beginning or end of a congressional or presidential term in order to strengthen or weaken the ability of constituents to link negative policy effects with legislators' votes. As a result, in developing extra-congressional procedures, legislators are likely to time the agent's action so that costs are less traceable and come in the "out" years.

Proposition III, Political Time—Legislative leaders must design their procedural path to conform to elite and public opinion, the institutional context in a given policy area, and the electoral calendar.

ତ୬ଡ

Some consensus among elites is a necessary precondition for Congress to act. The institutional context, as we will see, constrains or offers opportunities to legislative leaders deciding whether or not to delegate authority. Obviously, where institutions exist within the Congress that are capable of making these difficult decisions, legislators are less likely to delegate. In addition, the electoral calendar plays an important role in determining the set of politically feasible policy alternatives. That narrower set of politically feasible policy alternatives, in turn, narrows the field of potential procedural alternatives.

Proposition IV. Existence of Powerful Champions

Another potentially important factor in determining whether legislators will impose particularistic costs from within Congress or will delegate is whether there exist legislators who are well-positioned and interested enough to champion the cause. No observer would dispute that tax reform could never have moved forward in 1986 without the efforts of the Chairman of Ways and Means, Dan Rostenkowski (D-IL), and the Chairman of Finance, Bob Packwood (R-OR). The support of legislative leaders like these is, of course, desirable in shepherding any bill through the variety of obstacles the legislative process includes. However, because the deft manipulation of procedures is so critical to the enactment of the policies being examined here, the presence of well-placed supporters is an absolute precondition of handling these matters within Congress.

Proposition IV, Existence of Powerful Champions—Congress is more likely to delegate authority and employ an extra-congressional procedure when the legislative process offers no well-placed legislative leader willing to take the policy on as a priority.

Again, why such powerful champions are or are not attracted to these pieces of legislation is beyond the scope of this study and will be treated only peripherally.[15] What is relevant for our purposes is that tax reform attracted such well-placed individuals within Congress and base closure did not. Simply put, procedural choice was impacted by their existence or their absence in each case.

Proposition V. The One, the Few, and the Many

A final important factor we will consider is the number of particularistic groups that must bear the costs in the course of delivering general benefits. In tax reform, legislators sought to close a large number of tax loopholes favored by various groups whereas in siting a high-level waste repository, legislators sought to impose particularistic costs on one group—those who live near the site. This distinction is important because it suggests that, in these cases, the hurdle to be overcome in enacting such policies is higher or lower because of the sheer number of groups, and the size of those groups, in opposition.

Proposition V, The One, the Few, and the Many—The larger the number of groups that will suffer the particularistic pain, the more likely Congress is to delegate authority and employ an extra-congressional procedure.

In short, legislators would find it more difficult to site ten high-level nuclear waste repositories than one because it would require overcoming the objections of ten times as many obstructionist fellow legislators and groups. The difficulties of overcoming just one such group are substantial. Delegation becomes more and more attractive as the number of these groups multiplies.

Applying the Theory

Why Case Studies?

In chapters 2–5, the theory outlined above is applied to four cases in which Congress conferred general benefits while imposing some particularistic cost. A case-study method is most appropriate in applying the theory and testing these propositions for the first time. While it is clear that Congress is quite capable of enacting legislation that cuts particularistic benefits in favor of some general benefit, it is equally clear that the universe of cases under study is limited; far more limited, for instance, than if we were studying all legislation that confers general benefits or all legislation in which coalition leaders utilized unusual procedural mechanisms. Because we are examining relatively unusual cases, it is more appropriate to study a small number of cases in greater detail. In short, the quality of the theory advanced in the preceding pages is less likely to be answered reliably by crude quantitative measures than by the rich detail of particular cases.

Case Selection

While we can point to a significant number of cases in which legislators imposed particularistic costs on discrete groups in favor of general benefits over the last twenty-five years, in examining the question of procedural choice, it is useful to first distinguish between those in which the particularistic costs were relatively geographically concentrated and those in which the particularistic costs were relatively geographically dispersed. Table 1.1 illustrates a number of cases in which Congress was able to pass legislation that imposed direct, early-order costs on particular groups in favor of general benefits.

Because the geographic distinction is so prominent in the literature, it is important to be sure cases are selected with an eye toward the geographic dispersion of the particularistic benefits being cut or costs being imposed. More importantly, because the central question that motivates this study is that of procedural choice, cases must be chosen that provide some variance on that dimension. The cases selected for study are those arranged in Table 1.2 below.

The cases of tax reform and base closure thus serve as two cases that meet the hypothetical expectations of the first proposition discussed above. Because base closure requires imposing costs on relatively discrete geographic constituencies and because the literature tells us that the geographic nature of these costs makes them particularly sensitive, we expect members of Congress to have a great deal of difficulty in making these decisions internally. Therefore, it is not surprising to us to find that an extra-congressional procedure was utilized. Similarly, in the case of tax reform, we would expect internal procedures to be used. Because the particularistic benefits to be cut are less geographic in nature, Congress prefers to handle these matters internally.

Each of the other two cases fails to meet the solely geographic expectations of procedural choice. The case of nuclear waste disposal, like that of base closure, is one in which Congress seeks to impose geographically concentrated costs in favor of some general benefit. While we would expect an extra-congressional procedure to be utilized, the choice of a high-level

Table 1.1
Cases in Which Congress Imposes Direct, Early-Order Costs on Particular
Groups to Provide Benefits to a General, Diffuse Public

Geographically Concentrated Groups	Geographically Dispersed Groups
Choice of Nuclear Waste Disposal Site	Airline Deregulation
Line Item Veto	Tax Reform Act of 1986
Base Realignment and Closure	Social Security Reform
Commission	North American Free Trade Agreement

Table 1.2
Cases Selected for Study

	Geographically Concentrated	Geographically Dispersed
Internal Procedures	Choice of Nuclear Waste Disposal Site	Tax Reform Act of 1986
Extra-Congressional Procedures	Base Realignment and Closure Commission	North American Free Trade Agreement

nuclear waste disposal site was effectively[16] handled within Congress.
Similarly, the fast-track procedure utilized in the negotiation and approval
of the North American Free Trade Agreement (NAFTA) fails to meet the
expectation of this first proposition. Trade policy, like tax reform, clearly
imposes costs on geographically dispersed communities, thus suggesting that
Congress would be more inclined to handle the matter internally. In this
case, however, Congress appears to have delegated to a significant degree.

Conclusion

There are at least two compelling reasons why this question of procedural
choice deserves our attention. First, in describing the difference between distributive and informational theories of legislative organization, Keith Krehbiel
(1991, 7) points out that these two schools of thought "have distinctly different empirical implications at each of two observable levels of legislative
choice: the policies enacted by legislatures, and the institutions developed and

employed by legislatures." Since so few models of congressional policymaking account in any way for the passage of laws that confer general benefits while imposing particularistic costs, and since the development and employment of extra-congressional procedures appear to be avenues toward that end, these are observations that warrant explanations. When Congress repeatedly acts contrary to the conventional wisdom of at least a major part of the discipline, and does so using procedures that are new and unique, it is appropriate to ask in what ways our existing explanations are incomplete or inaccurate.

Second, and perhaps more importantly, the increasing use of extra-congressional procedures raises important normative questions that can be addressed only if we first understand why and when Congress chooses to use them. For instance, what will these procedures mean for the democratic accountability of our governing institutions? Do these procedures enhance the capacity of Congress to resist parochialism? While these are not the central questions to be addressed in this discussion, it is clear that these are important questions that *cannot* be answered unless we first have some understanding of why and when Congress chooses to employ extra-congressional procedures.

Concluding debate in the House of Representatives over the authorization of the base-closure commission process, Representative Richard Armey (R-TX) argued,

> the adventures of the base closing bill serve to demonstrate the strength of our system. Our cumbersome legislative procedures ensure not only that it is much harder to make a law than it is to prevent a law from being made, but that any bill that completes the complex dance of legislation has been thoroughly considered and deliberated. Over the last 2 years [1987–1988], every conceivable objection to this admittedly novel concept has been thoroughly ventilated. Every member with a legitimate concern has had a chance to be heard, and specific votes have been called and recorded on virtually every aspect.[17]

In this respect, Armey sounds much like Barbara Sinclair in arguing, correctly, that the dominant textbook understanding of how a bill becomes a law is dated, often inaccurate, and desperately in need of editing. The question to be asked and answered in this book suggests that at least one chapter in the new textbooks on Congress ought to be reserved for what are perhaps the most complex legislative dances of all—extra-congressional legislative procedures.

TWO

Base Closure

The problem of closing military bases presents a classic collective-action problem. Members have obvious electoral incentives to acquire military bases for their districts just as they regularly seek federal grants and construction projects. But members have even greater electoral incentives to ensure that benefits already acquired are maintained.[1] It is not surprising, then, that members are willing to fight tooth and nail to maintain military bases in their districts. Bases provide jobs both directly and indirectly to large numbers of constituents. Members fear these constituents will hold them personally responsible for their fate should they lose those jobs. The sum of all members fighting to maintain their bases means that Congress, utilizing the normal legislative process, is unable to shut down military bases even when most members agree we have too many. So how did Congress do the right thing?

The commission procedure eventually utilized to close military bases has taken two very similar forms. Under the procedure adopted in 1988,[2] Congress gave legal sanction to a commission that had already been established by Secretary of Defense Frank Carlucci to draw up a list of bases to be closed or realigned by December 31, 1988. The list would then be forwarded to the secretary of defense, who could either reject or accept the list without amendment. Congress retained the right to pass a joint resolution disapproving the list without amendments, but this effectively meant a two-thirds majority would be required to stop the list.[3] Significantly, the new procedure also exempted the commission and the Pentagon from complying with National Environmental Policy Act (NEPA) of 1969 environmental impact statement requirements, but did require compliance with NEPA requirements in closing and realigning bases. The NEPA requirements had been the main source of congressional delay and obstruction in attempted base closures since 1977.

There were only a few differences in the second procedure, adopted in 1990.[4] This procedure called for three additional rounds of base closures in

1991, 1993, and 1995. In these rounds, the secretary of defense was empowered to write the initial list and forward it to the commission, which would be empowered to add or delete bases. The list would then be forwarded to the president, who could approve or reject the list without amendments. Congress would again have the option of disapproving the list as a whole with a joint resolution. While in the first round the commission was forced to choose for closure only those bases whose savings would offset closing costs within six years, this requirement was dropped in the second procedure. A more automatic funding mechanism was also adopted in the second procedure to cut off the appropriations process as a potential back-door option for legislators hoping to keep their base open, and GAO review of commission calculations was also mandated in the second procedure. Finally, under the second procedure, appointment of commission members was to be subject to Senate confirmation.

From a public choice perspective, both procedures provide *a solution* to a classic collective-action problem. The question, however, is why *this particular solution?* Why didn't Congress, for instance, simply allow a committee to report legislation and consider the legislation under a closed rule in the House? Why didn't Congress delegate authority to the Pentagon to close bases? These questions can be answered only by first understanding the unique institutional and historical context surrounding military base closures. When the collective-action problem of base closures is placed within that context, it becomes clear that the base closure commission procedure represented the *only* politically feasible route to closing military bases in the 1980s and 1990s.

A Brief History of Military Base Closures

1789–1960

As Christopher J. Deering (1996, 155) points out, "the roots of the base closure controversy run deep in American history." Article I, Section 8 grants the Congress authority for the "erection of forts, magazines, arsenals, dockyards, and other needful buildings" and Article IV, Section 3 grants the Congress power to "dispose of and make all needful rules and regulations respecting the territory or other property" of the federal government.

As is the case with many powers granted to Congress, authority to construct and close bases was delegated to the executive. And like many other policy areas, Congress restricted, rather narrowly, executive authority for the construction and disposal of military facilities during peacetime and provided more liberal grants of power during wartime (Deering 1996, 155). One distinctive characteristic of military construction as a policy area, however, is its parochial nature. This led to relatively wide divergence in policy views between the legislative and executive branches in this particular part of defense policy. Because there are many communities which owe their growth and, in some cases, their very existence to the presence of a local military installation, the legislators who represent these military communities quickly became more ardent advocates and defenders of the activities undertaken on the base, and of the existence of the base itself, than any executive branch official. The classic expression of this remains the Armed Services Committee aide who pointed out to one researcher, "our committee is a real estate committee. Don't forget that. If you study our committee, you are studying real estate transactions."[5]

This line of thinking has been and remains the most important legacy of the early development of military installations policy. Arnold (1981b, 263) points out that the intensity and political sensitivity surrounding military installations policy is highlighted by the division of labor in the appropriations subcommittees of the House and Senate. Appropriations for the Department of Defense (DOD) are reported by two of these subcommittees. For fiscal 2003, the Subcommittee on Military Construction helped to enact (PL 107–249) a $10.5 billion bill to pay for new military construction. The Subcommittee on National Security (Armed Services in the Senate) helped to enact (PL 107–248) a $355.1 billion bill to pay for all other activities associated with the Defense Department. Moreover, for all the anger and resentment that President Clinton's use of the line-item veto aroused on Capitol Hill, only one package of rescissions was ever reinstated overriding the President's veto—a $286.7 million rescission package from a military construction appropriations bill.[6]

All this is significant, of course, because what matters most are the *perceptions* legislators have about the costs and benefits associated with legislative action. For instance, Arnold (1981b, 253, my emphasis) argues that

> the eventual impact of local benefits on congressional policy making depends crucially on how congressmen evaluate both the general and group costs and benefits associated with particular programs. Local benefits become paramount when congressmen *believe* that a program would have few general or group benefits, or considerable costs of either type.

In the case of base closure, the formative role the development of military installations policy plays in legislators' perceptions is therefore crucial.

Legislators who conceive of military installations policy in terms of the local benefits it delivers cannot be expected to receive notices of executive plans to close military bases with reticence.

1960–1970

The contemporary battle over base closures began with the Kennedy and Johnson administrations' initiatives to close bases between 1961 and 1965. Each year, the Pentagon released a new base closure list and each year the lists were extensive—73 bases in 1961, 98 bases in 1962, 33 bases in 1963, 95 bases in 1964, and 149 bases in 1965.[7] The congressional response was increasingly hostile. In May 1965, the House Armed Services Committee inserted a provision in the fiscal 1966 defense authorization bill providing for a one-house legislative veto of base closure plans and, after conference on the bill, a compromise provision was approved by both houses that imposed a variety of restrictions on Pentagon attempts to close bases. The restrictions included a mandatory 120-day delay between announcement and implementation of base closures. More importantly, the bill restricted the Pentagon to announcing closures between January 1 and April 30 so that the Armed Services Committees would have an opportunity to write language into defense authorization bills precluding the closure of bases the Congress did not want to close. President Johnson vetoed the bill in August 1965 on the grounds that it violated the separation of powers and the Congress did not attempt to override the president's veto. However, a new provision was passed delaying implementation of closures until thirty days after the Pentagon had provided the Armed Services Committees with a justification for closure decisions (Twight 1990, 242–43).

Despite this mini-revolt, the Pentagon had remarkable success closing bases during the 1960s. There was resistance from Congress, but that resistance generally took the form of legislators appealing directly to the Pentagon on behalf of bases, and legislators generally accepted even the Pentagon's adverse decisions (Hadwiger 1993, 91). If, as argued above, legislators viewed the construction, and even more so, the closure of military installations through local lenses, how is it that they allowed these closures to proceed with almost no systematic resistance? More specifically, why didn't legislators engage in the dilatory and obstructionist tactics they would employ just a decade later in response to base closures?

There are several reasons why Congress allowed closures to go forward, but the main reason was that the base closure policy process in the 1960s was merely reflective of what many other policy processes looked like during that decade—it was dominated by its own set of norms and practices consistent with a subgovernment model of policymaking. Members of Congress generally were more willing than today to defer to the expertise and objectivity of Pentagon analyses. Particularly during the early 1960s, the Pentagon retained widespread prestige and dominated the defense policy process. Moreover, this time arguably marked the height of the Cold War, so members of Congress were less willing to challenge Pentagon assessments about appropriate force posture. But another important factor in explaining the relative congressional complaisance on base closures was the cozy arrangement that had developed between members of the relevant military committees in Congress and the Pentagon. Arnold (1981a, 117) argues that "the evidence is compelling that bureaucrats avoided closing bases in districts with representatives on the military committees." David Casimir Hadwiger (1993, 89) concludes that although bases in important members' districts were closed, "Arnold is probably at least partially correct." In exchange for the courtesy paid to them by the Pentagon, the military committees gave relatively wide latitude to the Department of Defense on base closure.

1970–1976

This cozy arrangement began to break down in the late 1960s. During the first half of the next decade, four factors would converge to help construct a large bipartisan coalition against Pentagon base closure lists. First, Pentagon prestige was quickly eroding as the situation in Vietnam deteriorated. At the same time, Congress was rapidly developing its own sources of expertise and analysis. The number of staff members on both the House and Senate Armed Services Committees tripled between 1961 and 1976 (Hadwiger 1993, 92). Together, these developments meant that Congress would be less likely to defer to Pentagon expertise.

Second, Congress was undergoing its own rapid institutional change in this period. Kenneth Shepsle (1989) points out that the old equilibrium in which Congress was dominated by its full standing committees, and more specifically by the chairs of those committees, was being replaced by a new institutional dynamic in which rank-and-file members were becoming active players in greater numbers of policy areas. This decentralization of power meant not only that each member had more tools at his or her disposal to defend bases selected for closure in their districts, but also that members were less likely to display the kind of deference to the committee chairs of the relevant committees on base closure policy that had been the norm previously.[8]

Third, the particulars of the base closure lists of the early 1970s angered members of Congress. Many members came to believe that closure lists were politically motivated, that the Pentagon selected for closure bases in the districts of members who were uncooperative with the administration, that it was complicit in hiding information and actively deceiving members of Congress, and that the savings from base closures were not nearly as large as the Pentagon claimed.[9] Looking back on the imposition of restrictions on Pentagon closure plans in 1976 and 1977, Senator Carl Levin (D-MI) argued,

> the origin of the congressional restrictions on base closings, which we basically have retained in the law over the years, is what happened in Massachusetts in the early 1970s. Massachusetts was the only state to vote Democratic in 1972 and what happened in 1974? President Nixon's Pentagon came up with a list of bases to be closed, and Massachusetts was disproportionately and heavily impacted by that list. . . . Let me remind my colleagues that there was a reason for this protection. This country is based on a premise that we do not want all power in one branch of Government. There was too much power for the executive branch to unilaterally close bases, and Congress did something about it.[10]

Finally, deteriorating economic conditions in the nation as a whole, and in the Northeast and Midwest in particular, made members of Congress much more sensitive to the economic impact of closures (Hadwiger 1993, 88). When the Pentagon released a base closure list in April 1973 that included 274 separate realignment and closure actions, there was a widespread belief that the actions disproportionately fell on those districts in the Northeast. Shortly before the list was released, a group of predominantly northeastern legislators proposed legislation for an independent commission to review base closure proposals from the Pentagon (Hadwiger 1993, 70–73). The release of the list fanned the flames of discontent in Congress and, though the legislation never passed either house, it served as a formative period for the coalition that would eventually impose real restrictions on Pentagon closure plans.

With roughly five hundred bases closed during the early 1970s (*Congressional Quarterly* 1989), the Pentagon's announcement of 147 additional closures in March and April 1976 became the straw that broke the camel's back. Led by House Majority Leader Tip O'Neill (D-MA) and Representative William Cohen (R-ME), who was enraged by the inclusion of Loring Air Force Base in central Maine on the most recent list of closures, Congress attached restrictive provisions to the military construction bill. It required notification when bases were candidates for closure, a mandatory waiting period of nine months, DOD compliance with NEPA requirements, a

detailed justification of decisions to proceed with closure, and a 90-day waiting period after a decision was made by DOD to close a base in order to allow
Congress to block a closure if it so desired. President Ford vetoed the measure
despite strong sentiment in Congress for an override. The House did eventually override the veto, but the Senate fell short. Despite this failure, Congress
eventually passed and the president signed a nearly identical version of the bill.
The only significant change was that the one-year delay in implementation of
closures was shortened to sixty days, but the change was effectively meaning-
less because compliance with NEPA requirements would still take a year.
Though this legislation was only effective for one year, a nearly identical provision was passed a year later, which made the procedural changes permanent.
Moreover, while the original legislation applied only to military installations
employing over five hundred people, it was amended in 1978 to cover all military installations employing over three hundred (Twight 1990, 244–45).

1977–1988

The new base closure procedure effectively stopped base closures cold.
When Secretary of Defense Harold Brown proposed base closures and
realignments in 1978 and 1979, he was completely frustrated. Charlotte
Twight (1990, 246) outlines the difficulty:

> Congress now had a profusion of tools with which to undercut proposed
> base closures: NEPA court challenges, Congressional hearings on the can-
> didate bases and on the detailed justifications DOD submitted,
> Congressional demands for environmental studies during the authoriza-
> tion and appropriation process even when not otherwise required by law,
> denial of design funds for base consolidation, disapproval of construction
> funds to effect closures or realignments, imposition of requirements for
> alternate use studies or one-year delays prior to implementation, and
> "remedial" legislation to block entirely DOD's decision to close or
> realign a military base. These tools were employed with zeal.

Congress's victory on the issue was total. No major base—not one—was
closed in the period between 1977 and 1988, while thirteen were created
(*Congressional Quarterly* 1989). Moreover, the Reagan administration's
homeport project, which effectively spread out the home ports for the navy,
made closures even more difficult politically by expanding the number of legislators with something to defend. Minor revisions were made to base closure
procedures in 1982 and 1985, but the net effect was negligible.

What changed, then, in the late 1980s to make base closure politically viable again in the Congress? First, the budget deficit had become a politically salient issue and members were increasingly searching for votes to bolster their deficit-hawk credentials. Second, the thaw in relations between East and West meant that many members of Congress were beginning to look at the large defense budget as a potential source of spending cuts. Third, as we will see, the late 1980s offered a unique window of political opportunity that would make base closure easier for members to swallow.

Whatever the changed political atmosphere was, however, one thing was sure. A successful base closure procedure would have to be sensitive to the historical and institutional developments of the preceding quarter century. Members could not be expected to defer to executive expertise or prestige, and the rise of the more individualized political enterprises in Congress meant that the new process would somehow have to be insulated from the meddling of individual legislators without entirely delegating away key institutional prerogatives. As we will see, only the base closure commission procedure met all these requirements.

Applying the Theory: Procedural Choice and Base Closures

The congressional debate over the base closure commission procedure reveals a variety of ways in which the unique procedure satisfied the many congressional concerns regarding base closure. While the geographic nature of the particularistic cost being imposed and the scope of the policy area were critical factors in the choice of an extra-congressional procedure, it is also clear that the institutional developments in this policy area outlined above served as another critical set of factors in procedural choice. In short, an extra-congressional procedure made sense in the case of base closure because of the sensitive nature of the particularistic cost and also because the policy area in question provided a relatively cost-free avenue of delegation. But the unique form of delegation legislative leaders concocted is evidence of the importance of historical context in understanding procedural choice.

Proposition I. Geographic Concentration of Costs

Perhaps no other concern has been more widely cited and discussed in the difficulty surrounding base closure than the fact that the benefits from military installations are shared by concentrated geographic groups.[11] As discussed earlier, this means not only that these groups have direct representation in both houses of Congress, but also that they are more likely to organize in opposition to a base closure as a result of their geographic proximity.[12]

One piece of evidence suggesting the importance of geography is the fact that base closures have always been a matter of much greater sensitivity in the House with its smaller constituencies than in the Senate (Twight 1990, 241). This difference in comparative sensitivity is perhaps best revealed by the way the two houses reacted to Secretary of Defense Dick Cheney's attempt to unilaterally close bases in 1990. Cheney proposed a list of forty-seven bases to close early in that year. In response, the Senate Armed Services Committee version of the 1991 Defense Authorization bill included provisions to remove some of the procedural hurdles to base closure in place since 1976. The House, on the other hand, adopted procedures designed to preclude *any* base closures, even those that would have been allowed under the O'Neill-Cohen procedures, until Cheney offered legislation establishing a nonpartisan base closure procedure (*Congressional Quarterly* 1993, 353–54).

The problem of geography was so pervasive in the case of base closures that no major base had been closed in the United States under the O'Neill-Cohen procedures mainly because individual members of Congress were very active in blocking base closures in their districts. As Twight (1990, 250) points out, "it is the perceived duty of every senator and representative to block military base closures or reductions in his or her state or district within the bounds of existing law. Constituents demand it; reelection requires it." The result was that, by 1988, actively blocking the closure of a military base no longer provided any reward for legislators. It was expected and required of them. The new commission procedure, on the other hand, "might expand such credit-claiming opportunities" (Twight 1990, 276 n44) by allowing members to become heroic advocates for bases on the closure list. In frequently cited remarks, Senator Phil Gramm (R-TX) outlines the political rationale:

> The beauty of this proposal is that: If you have a military base in your district—God forbid one should be closed in Texas, but it could happen—under this proposal, I have sixty days. So I come up here and I say, "God have mercy. Don't close this base in Texas. We can get attacked from the south. The Russians are going to go after our leadership and you know they are going to attack Texas. We need this base. Then I can go out and lie down in the street and the bulldozers are coming and I have a trusty aide there just as it gets there to drag me out of the way. All the people in Muleshoe, or wherever this base is, will say, "You know, Phil Gramm got whipped, but it was like the Alamo. He was with us until the last second."[13]

Many others were equally explicit about the way in which the commission procedure would free members of Congress from blame for the loss of geographic benefits. Arguing for the political logic of a congressional vote of disapproval rather than Congress having to vote to approve the base closure list from the commission, Representative John Kasich (R-OH) argues,

> I think it makes far greater sense from a political perspective for yourselves not to be held responsible for being able to stop a bill from coming up. It is much easier to be able to make the argument that, "I tried to get a resolution of disapproval, but the Congress just simply wouldn't buy it."[14]

Both Kasich's and Gramm's comments above suggest a similar logic, then. Legislators could break the chain of traceability[15] between their actions and the negative policy impacts of base closure. Indeed both Kasich and Gramm go beyond mere blame avoidance to suggest the new procedure would open new credit-claiming opportunities; legislators could play the role of tragic hero for their constituents.

Attractive as this logic is, however, it does not deal with the difficulties of delegation. How would the costs of delegation be contained? To whom should Congress delegate?

Proposition II. Scope of the Policy Area

Representative Richard Armey (R-TX) was the main sponsor and the driving force in the Congress behind the commission procedure. He had nearly succeeded in attaching the procedure to the defense authorization bill in 1987, coming just seven votes short. Armey believed that the key to the base closure issue was to view it through an institutional lens. Speaking of the O'Neill-Cohen procedures, Armey (1988, 73) argued, "one can speculate on whether or not the Maine delegation had parochial motives in stopping base closings with red tape, but they would never have been able to sell it to the Congress as a purely parochial concern." The real issue, he argued, was the legislative-executive battle:

> At issue is who will have control of the pork. Any congressional veteran will tell you that pork is power—both the ability to distribute it and the ability to deny it. If the executive branch has unrestricted freedom to close bases, the argument runs, it would have a potent political weapon in its hands to retaliate against anyone who defies the president on key legislation. Congress has an institutional interest in insuring that the

executive branch does not have it. And while parochial interests can be defeated, . . . institutional interests cannot.[16]

Armey knew, then, that a base closure procedure would be adopted only if it could address this problem of delegation.

Opponents of the commission procedure knew this too, and they went to great pains to depict this delegation of power as apocalyptic. Senator Alan Dixon (D-IL), the primary opponent of the legislation in the Senate, argued,

> I do not know, in my professional career, which spans now almost four decades, any kind of exceptional authority as immense, as dramatic, as overwhelming, as undemocratic as the provision in this bill that will permit the Secretary of Defense to appoint a commission of people of his choice to bring back to him a list of bases to be closed, and, boom, they are closed and Congress has nothing to say.[17]

Representative Frank Horton (R-NY) referred to Armey's bill as "the largest unbridled delegation of legislative authority in the history of this country,"[18] and Senator Levin referred to it as "an excessive delegation of power. It is not in keeping with our celebration of the Constitution, which calls for divided power."[19]

Meanwhile, both sides of the debate outlined the dangers of allowing for any "political" influence over base closure decisions, whether it comes from Congress, the Pentagon, or the White House. Senator William Cohen took to the Senate floor to explain that it was the constant stonewalling of information from the air force regarding the proposed closure of Loring Air Force Base in Maine that had led him to become a sponsor of the restrictive base closure legislation in 1976 and 1977.[20] Representative Jim Kolbe (R-AZ) pointed out that the "most important" aspect of a base closure procedure must be that "the executive branch will not be able to make arbitrary or capricious decisions."[21] Representative Armey reiterated his view that the "larger concern" in base closure is the interest of the institution:

> Historically, base closing has been used as a point of leverage by administrations, both Republican and Democratic administrations, as political leverage over and above Members of Congress to encourage them to vote in a manner that the administration would like. So we have communities afflicted, and we have seen, I am afraid, even base closings that would hamper our nation's defense out of a sense of political interest.[22]

This institutional problem was so sensitive, in fact, that during the congressional debate many members raised concerns about the lack of independence of the commission and its staff. An opponent of the commission process, Representative Porter pointed out that the Armey bill would simply be providing legal sanction to base closure efforts already underway by Secretary of Defense Frank Carlucci:

> The Secretary of Defense has chartered a commission which presently is comprised of his appointees, staffed by his staffers, receives information from his offices, will report directly to him, and whose recommendations will probably lead to the closing or realigning of a number of military installations. All of that without any congressional input.[23]

Porter eventually proposed an amendment barring anyone from serving on the commission staff who had been employed by the Pentagon within the past year.[24]

In light of these institutional concerns, it is not hard to imagine why the commission process was politically attractive. Congress would delegate authority to propose base closures to an ad hoc institution and force the executive to close only those bases approved by the independent commission or close none at all. But as with most great works of art, the beauty of the commission process as a solution to the institutional problem of delegation was most evident in the details.

Kenneth Mayer (1995, 395) points out that members of Congress made sure to limit "the domain of the agent's authority" by establishing decision-making criteria for the commission; establishing membership controls over the commission; and, most importantly for our purposes, restricting the jurisdictional scope of the commission's deliberations. The decision-making criteria imposed upon the commission both limited the range of candidates for closure and forced the creation of a written record, which could later be subjected to analysis by other independent organizations such as the GAO. Mayer (1995, 400–401) provides an example of how the criteria limited the commission's discretion:

> One criteria [sic] imposed on the 1988 commission, but dropped thereafter, was a requirement that all costs of any one base closure be recovered within six years. The origin of the requirement was a mystery; it was added to the 1988 bill by the House Armed Services Committee, but nobody outside of the committee—not even the commission itself—knew who had inserted it or why it was there. The provision meant that the

commission could not close any large bases because it was impossible to quickly recover the huge costs of shutting down a major installation (transfer of military personnel, upgrading facilities elsewhere, property disposal, etc.) and the shutdown itself might take several years.

Congress also exerted control over the membership of the commission and its staff. Under the 1990 procedure, the president could appoint members of the commission, but the nominees were subject to Senate confirmation. In the first round, Congress required that half the commission staff had to be people who had not held positions within the Department of Defense within the past year. In the 1990 law, the level was raised to two-thirds, and requirements were added specifying that no Defense Department employee could serve as a lead analyst on commission research and that Defense Department employees who had previously worked on base closure issues within the Pentagon could not serve on the staff (Mayer 1995, 402).

Finally, and most importantly, Congress also limited the commission's discretion by limiting its jurisdiction. Many members of Congress fought to allow the commission to consider overseas bases for closure. Representative Jon Kyl (R-AZ) argued that foreign bases should not be included because "it is going to muddle the thing up, it is going to complicate it so much that we are really not going to accomplish the first task we set out to accomplish."[25] Armey pointed out that foreign bases had to be omitted in order to prevent

> this commission from being sort of sucked into what might be, from a decision-making point of view, a bottomless pit of international relations and a number of considerations of foreign policy and international treaties that take us far beyond the original scope of this bill.[26]

But this was more than just a matter of making life easier for the commissioners. Members of Congress were very much interested, as Mayer (1995, 404) points out, in limiting the ability of the commission "to make judgments and trade-offs that crossed any issue boundaries." Provisions were added in 1990, for instance, that prohibited the commission from looking at facilities that were not under the direct control of the Department of Defense, so that facilities under the control of the Army Corps of Engineers could be protected (Mayer 1995, 405).

It is clear, then, that the scope of the policy area played a central role in procedural choice in the case of base closures. The amendment to include foreign bases in the commission's purview has obvious political appeal.

Members could then vote to cut the deficit, improve defense posture, and know that at least some of the costs (and hopefully most of them) would be borne by nobody's district. Despite this inherent appeal, the amendment failed by wide margins in both houses. Why? Because members obviously perceived more political danger in allowing the agent (in this case, the commission) to influence a larger number of issues in other policy areas than they saw in simply rolling the dice and allowing for the potential of the commission closing bases in their own districts.

Thus, the variety of ways in which members of Congress were able to limit the discretion of the commission goes a long way toward explaining why Congress utilizes extra-congressional procedures in the case of base closures and does not do so in broader policy areas such as tax reform. The delegation of authority to implement particularistic cuts is simply not a politically realistic possibility in the case of broad policy areas because, by definition, it would be impossible to limit the jurisdiction of the agent in the way this was done in base closure.

Proposition III. Political Time

The case of base closure also points to the importance of each of the three factors that relate to political time mentioned in the first chapter. First, it is absolutely clear that by the late 1980s, most members of Congress, in addition to elites in the Pentagon and the White House, believed that there were too many military bases and that closing military bases could both improve force posture and save money at a time when deficits were a significant concern.

Second, the procedural vehicle eventually used is a result of the institutional evolution within the policy area over time. That members of Congress view the construction and closure of military bases through a parochial lens has as much to do with the ways in which military bases were first built—remember that these decisions are sealed off in a separate subcommittee from all other defense decisions—as it does with the nature of the policy area or the geographic concentration of the benefit. In addition, we have also seen that the perceived political abuse of base closures by the Pentagon and the White House in the 1970s was a major reason why members restricted the Pentagon's power to unilaterally close military bases in the late 1970s. In attempting to close military bases a decade later, coalition leaders had to be sensitive to this historical context. Effectively, this meant that certain procedural options were not politically feasible. Specifically, delegation of authority to the president or the Pentagon to unilaterally draw up a list of bases to be closed was understood by all to be unacceptable.

Much of the congressional literature deals directly with the development of social norms, practices, and patterns of behavior that help to structure conflict within the institution. While those norms certainly owe their existence, in part, to rational actors seeking to structure conflict within a large and diverse body, they also are the result of the outcomes of previous conflicts and resolutions. So while other factors explain why Congress cannot handle base closure internally, this historical context serves as the primary reason legislators needed to develop the unique extra-congressional procedure they did.

Finally, it is important to note that the base closure commission process was also very much a product of the electoral calendar. Any piece of legislation that cuts particularistic benefits or imposes particularistic costs can realistically be adopted only if it finds some way to obscure the causal chain between the votes of legislators and the negative policy effects. It is this notion, after all, that leads legislators to utilize procedural tactics in the first place. In this light, there are a variety of reasons why the commission process was more attractive to legislators in 1988 than it had been in 1987, or 1973 (the first time it had been proposed) for that matter.

For example, legislation authorizing the first round of closures was passed shortly before Election Day in 1988, when voters and, more importantly, challengers, would know that the incumbent had voted to close bases generally, but would have no idea which bases were going to be closed. The specific base closure list was to be released after Election Day, on December 31, and there was a requirement that no closures would be implemented prior to 1990. This meant that by the time the economic pinch of base closures was being felt by constituents, there would be several years, a round of redistricting, and at least a couple of elections between any legislator's vote for base closure and the potentially negative policy effects of those closures (Mayer 1995, 406).

The 1990 law, which called for three additional rounds of base closures, in 1991, 1993, and 1995, displayed a similar temporal sensitivity. First, it called for three rounds of closures at once, limiting the number of votes legislators would have to cast to close bases. Second, it added an extra round of base closures before members would be running for office in their new district boundaries in 1992. Finally, closures would be announced in the middle of nonelection years, allowing members in affected districts time to contain the political damage.

But just as important as all these features was the political timing of the original base closure procedure. During the congressional debate, Representative Dickinson pointed out that

the fact is that many circumstances have come together to make it possible in this short window to pass this legislation now. It is my opinion that
if we do not pass this bill and allow these base closures to be named this
year, we will be another ten years before such an opportunity comes
again. We have a lame duck Congress, we have a lame duck administration, we have a lame duck Secretary of Defense, all of whom support this
legislation.[27]

In later debate, Dickinson added, "all these things come into alignment at the
same time, and this adds to the credibility of the bill."[28] Representative Joel
Hefley (R-CO) explained that the timing was politically safe because "the
commission would report after Election Day and the Secretary would have to
act before Inauguration Day."[29]

In short, there was something special about 1988 as a moment on the electoral calendar that made the vote to close bases far easier than it would have
been otherwise. That it was a unique moment is undisputable. The rare dou-
ble play of a lame duck administration and congressional redistricting directly on the horizon had occurred only a very few other times in the twentieth
century when an extra-congressional procedure was arguably unnecessary
for base closure.[30] The point here is that the particular moment on the electoral calendar offers constraints and opportunities to coalition leaders that
played a role in procedural choice as well.

Proposition IV. Existence of Powerful Champions

The unique political sensitivity of base closure is further underscored by the
intense debate surrounding congressional involvement in commission deliberations. During that debate, Representative John Porter (R-IL) proposed an
amendment that would have included the chairmen and ranking members of
the relevant military committees as ex-officio members of the commission.
Without hesitation, Representatives Les Aspin (D-WI) and William
Dickinson (R-AL), the chair and ranking member of the House Armed
Service Committee, fought the amendment. Aspin argued, "I have enough
trouble getting myself elected as chairman of this committee in the caucus
over here every two years."[31] Dickinson added, "I would not like to serve on
[the commission]. I do not think the gentleman from California [Mr.
Dellums] or the gentleman from New York [Mr. Martin] are chomping at the
bit or wish to serve on it."[32]

The amendment was defeated by a voice vote; its easy defeat underscores
the rationale for utilizing an extra-congressional procedure to deal with

base closure rather than more common internal procedures such as closed rules and omnibus legislative vehicles. While Congress has been able to craft other pieces of legislation that cut particularistic benefits in favor of some general benefit, such as the Tax Reform Act of 1986, this could be accomplished only because there was some legislator or group of legislators willing to champion that legislation. Because of the geographic concentration of the costs associated with base closure, however, it is clearly impossible to attract a champion of *specific* closures. It is not surprising, then, that the delegation of authority became an attractive alternative to handling base closure internally.

Proposition V. The One, the Few, and the Many

Along these same lines, it is useful to think for a moment about the simple legislative mathematics of the base closure procedure. In theory, the Congress had a variety of alternative paths available in its attempt to close bases. If they had chosen to handle the matter within Congress, they could have closed one base at a time. The problem with this, of course, is not only that no legislator wants to be seen as attacking another member's parochial interests, but also that the general benefit from such a small policy proposal would be unlikely to generate the necessary enthusiasm to overcome the variety of veto points any bill must overcome. As the number of bases to be closed increases, on the other hand, the general benefits of base closure become more attractive, but the strength and anger of those legislators hurt by the base closures expands exponentially. In short, the general benefit does not become large enough to attract powerful champions and enthusiasm among the rank and file until enough bases are included that the group of legislators on the short end of the stick is too great and too powerful in a legislative process characterized by multiple veto points.

The procedure eventually employed recognizes this simple mathematics and makes it work to the advantage of those seeking closures. Both procedures called upon legislators to authorize base closures prior to finding out which bases would be closed. While some legislators[33] had more cause for concern than others, all could at least reasonably hope that no base in their district would be closed. Once the commission's list was released, on the other hand, the legislative mathematics had already turned against those with bases on the list.

The number of legislative districts forced to swallow the particularistic pain thus played an important role in procedural choice as well. In enacting a policy in which *many* districts must endure particularistic costs in favor of some general benefits, an extra-congressional procedure is clearly preferred by all concerned.

Doing the Right Thing: Did It Work?

Of course, all this was empty symbolism if it did not work. We have seen that Congress decided to move action on base closures out of Congress because the sensitivity of the geographically concentrated costs and the large number of legislators that might suffer electorally because of those costs were such that no well-placed legislative leader was willing to shepherd base closure through the regular legislative process. As a result, Congress created a new, ad hoc, institution with a remarkably limited jurisdictional authority to avoid the problems that attend delegation. We have also seen that Congress timed the procedure so as to further obscure the causal chain between legislators' votes in favor of base closure and the policy effects of base closure. But did it work? Were bases closed? Was money saved?

In most cases, it is difficult to answer these questions because one cannot prove the counterfactual. We cannot say with certainty what would have happened in the absence of the commission procedures. On the other hand, one is hard pressed to find a single political commentator or political actor who believes that the commission process did not result in more closures than would have been the case otherwise.

In the first round, 86 bases[34] were slated for closure and in the second, third, and fourth rounds, another 246 bases.[35] Many other bases, of course, were slated for realignments, which led to job losses in some cases and job gains in others. The amount of money actually saved from these closures is a matter of some dispute, as the total estimated savings depends on what is counted. The Department of Defense (1995, 1–3) excluded both environmental cleanup costs and the projected revenue from land sales from its calculations, and estimated that the total savings of the four rounds together would be $56.7 billion over twenty years. In rejecting calls for another round of base closures, on the other hand, many members of Congress argued that the four rounds had not generated as much in savings as the Pentagon and the commission claimed (Richter 1997, A19). Even these critics, however, do not dispute the fact that money is being saved as a result of base closures, regardless of how savings are calculated.

Another measure of the success of the commission process is the fact that there were relatively few attempts to circumvent the process to keep bases on the commission lists open and the few attempts that did occur were largely unsuccessful. Hadwiger (1993, 195) suggests that, in the first round at least, many of the bases closed were unpopular within their districts. While legislators could not be seen to stand idly by while the Pentagon closed these bases, they could allow the bases to be closed if their hands were effectively tied. In any event, there is some empirical evidence to suggest that the reason for the muted response was that legislators correctly determined that the base closures would not be decisive factors in their reelection efforts.[36]

There were many cases, however, where the response was not muted. Senator Dixon, described as "the Senate's most vocal opponent of the base-closing panel's mandate,"[37] planned hearings to "grill Pentagon base-closing staffers."[38] Others planned to circumvent the commission process by fighting to block the appropriations necessary to go forward with base closures.[39] Senator Arlen Specter (R-PA) challenged the closure of the Philadelphia Naval Shipyard in court and took his case all the way to the U.S. Supreme Court. Though there were cases of a few jobs being saved in very few cases,[40] legislators were otherwise completely unsuccessful in keeping targeted bases open.

Another possible indicator of the commission process's success was its ability to co-opt some of its strongest victims and detractors. For instance, Representative Jim Courter (R-NJ) served as the chair of the commission for its second and third rounds. Though Courter supported the commission process, he was a strenuous and vociferous opponent of the list that emerged from the first round of the commission process (Palmer 1991). That list called for the closure of Fort Dix, a major base in New Jersey, and on April 18, 1989, less than two years before he was appointed as chair of the second commission by President Bush, Courter voted for the joint resolution seeking to overturn the base closure recommendations in the House.

Senator Dixon, as we have seen, was the primary opponent of the commission process in the Senate in 1988, telling one reporter, "You've got to understand. This process was designed to stop a guy like me."[41] He fought vigorously to keep Chanute Air Force Base in Illinois open after it was recommended for closure in the first round of the commission process, declaring its closure "an American tragedy."[42] Nevertheless, Dixon accepted the appointment as the chair of the commission for its fourth round of closures.

Without a doubt, however, the greatest conversion on the issue of military base closures is that of William Cohen. No sooner was Cohen, the author of the legislative provisions in 1976 and 1977 that made it so difficult for the Pentagon to close military bases in the first place, named secretary of defense than he was calling for additional rounds of base closure. Sounding like a member of the base closure choir, Cohen said:

What I've told my former colleagues is that there aren't any more easy choices. Those are all gone. It's hemlock time now. Are you going to protect these excess facilities that are no longer needed, or are you going to protect our forces by putting modern weapons in their hands?[43]

Cohen reiterated this call a year later, asking for additional rounds of closures in 2001 and 2005 (Schafer 1998). In the FY2003 Defense Authorization Bill, Congress authorized one round of closures in 2005.

Conclusion

The last round of the commission process led to nearly as much anger and resentment within Congress as there had been in 1976. President Clinton privatized jobs in Texas and California that were supposed to have been shifted to bases in other states. In the wake of this action, Armey, then the Majority Leader in the House, suggested,

They [members of Congress] could overcome their fear of losing a base as long as they thought they had a fair shake in the matter. But the president poisoned the well badly. . . . You cannot have a commission, you cannot have closures without trust and confidence. . . . It's my honest assessment that you will not have another commission as long as Bill Clinton is in the White House and the reason is that, no matter how much he pleads that this time he will play it straight, they won't believe it.[44]

This view reemphasizes the argument made in this chapter. Congress will not close bases itself because of the geographic nature of the particularistic costs involved. Congress will not delegate authority to the Pentagon or the president to close bases unilaterally because of the history of base closures—a history that has now apparently been reinforced. Today, military bases can be closed only with a procedure that delegates authority, temporarily, to an institution independent of the executive, and only with a procedure sensitive to the political calendar. In short, the story of base closures teaches us that extra-congressional procedures can empower Congress *to do what it simply cannot do otherwise*.[45] In this case at least, extra-congressional procedures helped the Congress to "do the right thing."

Additional questions about extra-congressional procedures remain, however. For instance, the case of base closures raises interesting new questions about Congress's use of an extra-congressional procedure (fast-track procedures) in trade policy. The congressional debate surrounding base closures clearly indicates that one reason members of Congress were comfortable delegating the extraordinary authority they did, was because of the narrow nature of the policy area. This is clearly not the case with trade policy; NAFTA illustrates the wide range of policy areas trade policy affects.

Similarly, a deeper understanding of the story of base closures raises our level of curiosity about the case of nuclear waste disposal. On the surface, at least, these two cases appear to have much in common. They are both cases in which Congress is seeking to impose geographically concentrated costs in favor of some general benefit. Moreover, they are both very narrow policy areas, suggesting delegation of authority as a possibility since the jurisdiction of the agent could be restricted quite easily. Why, then, did legislators not utilize an extra-congressional procedure in the case of nuclear waste disposal? We respond to this question in the next chapter.

THREE

Nuclear Waste Disposal

Site selection for a high-level nuclear waste facility presents a policy problem that is very similar to base closure. In closing military installations, legislators are faced with the prospect of imposing significant, geographically concentrated costs on specific districts in favor of a general, diffuse benefit.[1] In that case, we saw that because of the political sensitivity of these geographically concentrated costs, legislators chose to delegate authority to close bases while restricting the scope of that delegation and maintaining the power to stop the base closure process. With this political logic in mind, then, one might expect legislators to behave similarly in choosing a site for a national nuclear waste dump rather than serve as the author or supporter of legislation that dumped highly toxic radioactive waste in a particular fellow legislator's district.

As we will see, however, while Congress appeared to delegate some authority in this case, the reality is that Congress, led by powerful and well-placed members, did ultimately make this choice itself. In adopting the 1982 Nuclear Waste Policy Act (Public Law 97–425) and the 1987 amendments to that law as part of the fiscal 1988 reconciliation bill (Public Law 100–203), Congress narrowed its sights and eventually singled out Yucca Mountain, Nevada as the sole site for a permanent repository designed to house high-level nuclear waste for thousands of years. Before examining the question of why Congress chose to handle this policy problem internally and how it did so, it is important to first understand the scope and history of the policy problem. After a very brief history of nuclear waste policy, we will examine the particular procedures employed to narrow the choices to Yucca Mountain and apply the theory of procedural choice developed earlier to the case of the Yucca Mountain Project.

A Brief History of Nuclear Waste Policy

A Primer on the Nuclear Fuel Cycle

Before launching into an analysis of nuclear waste policy, it is appropriate to have a minimal understanding of the particular kind of nuclear waste with which we are concerned in this chapter and how that nuclear waste is generated. This study is concerned only with spent fuel and, for reasons that will become clear later on, mostly with spent fuel that is generated from civilian commercial reactors.

According to the Nuclear Energy Institute, roughly 20 percent of the nation's electricity is generated by commercial nuclear reactors.[2] In a reactor, uranium contained in fuel rods undergoes the process of nuclear fission, producing heat. This heat produces steam that generates electricity. Over time, fuel rods become less efficient as the chain reaction within them is slowed despite the fact that they remain highly radioactive. After three or four years, spent fuel rods, which are contained in large fuel assemblies, are removed and stored in cooling pools of water or air-cooled dry casks. The problem with this is that these methods of storage are only meant to be temporary. Many of the sites at which the spent fuel is stored are near lakes, rivers, and urban populations and the spent fuel is dispersed throughout the country, with most states having at least some.

Remarkably few alternatives for the disposal of this waste have emerged. The main focus of federal nuclear waste disposal has been the concept of permanent geologic disposal. A 1957 National Academy of Sciences report to the Atomic Energy Commission recommended the burial of high-level waste in deep, stable rock formations; in particular, it suggested further research into formations known as salt beds and salt domes. Since then, research has been conducted on such salt formations along with volcanic rock formations (basalt and tuff) and crystalline rock formations (granite). The central idea behind permanent geologic disposal is to find a rock formation that is stable, that will retard the flow of groundwater through a disposal site, and that will be able to absorb as much of the radioactive material released as possible if groundwater does penetrate the repository (League of Women Voters 1993, 42–43). In addition to these natural barriers, a permanent geologic repository would also have artificially engineered barriers. However, it is important to note that spent fuel needs to be isolated for tens of thousands of years. As a result, the concerns with permanent geologic disposal include long-term issues such as climactic and seismic change at the site and the possibility of accidental or purposeful human intrusion into the repository.

One alternative to permanent geologic disposal is the reprocessing of spent fuel. When uranium undergoes fission in a reactor, plutonium is created which can then be used to generate more energy. There are two problems with reprocessing this spent fuel, however. First, reprocessing does not make financial sense for utilities because of the worldwide abundance of uranium. Second, and more importantly, plutonium can potentially be separated from the fuel and used in the construction of nuclear weapons, thus raising national security concerns. As a result, reprocessing is not used in the United States (League of Women Voters 1993, 39).

With disposal as the only choice, a number of alternatives to permanent geologic disposal have been considered and all but abandoned by the federal government. The most actively researched of these is sub-seabed disposal—disposal in sediments below 3,000 to 5,000 meters of ocean water. Significant uncertainties remain about sub-seabed disposal, including water flow through the sediments and the effect that the heat generated by waste packages would have on the surrounding sediment. A proposal to bury the waste in the Antarctic ice sheet never got off the ground because of uncertainty about the stability of the ice cap over thousands of years. Proposals to launch the waste into space have been abandoned because of both the cost of such a proposal and the possibility of a launch accident. Finally, some have suggested that spent fuel should either remain where it is in the short term or be transferred to a temporary away-from-reactor or monitored-retrievable-storage facility until a more technologically sound alternative emerges (League of Women Voters 1993, 44–46). These latter alternatives remain the only viable ones to permanent geologic disposal and will be discussed in greater detail later in this chapter.

Nuclear Waste Policy Prior to NWPA

The short version of the history of nuclear waste policy is that its history prior to the Nuclear Waste Policy Act (NWPA) is short. As Gerald Jacob (1990, 26) points out, 1954 was a milestone year in the beginning of nuclear waste policy. The 1954 Atomic Energy Act discarded provisions in the 1946 Atomic Energy Act that kept reactor-design data classified and encouraged the commercial development of nuclear power. The new law provided subsidies such as financing and the necessary fuel to firms willing to set up nuclear reactors that would generate electricity. The most important of these subsidies from the perspective of this study, however, was that the act required the

Atomic Energy Commission (AEC) to take responsibility for the reprocessing or disposal of the spent fuel from commercial reactors.

As was the case with military installations policy, nuclear energy policy in the 1950s and 1960s was characterized by a subgovernment type of politics. Jacob (1990, 27) argues,

> the 1954 act maintained federal preemption of the authority to regulate the nuclear industry, freeing utilities from pesky state regulations that could interfere with their operations. The AEC's relationship with Congress was generally benign. The Joint Committee on Atomic Energy (JCAE) monopolized congressional oversight and, with few exceptions, supported and promoted the AEC's mission. The AEC was both regulator and promoter of atomic energy and for years no other federal, let alone state, entity threatened its authority. Growth of the industry and advancement of nuclear power was accomplished by administrative fiat. The goals and policies of the promotional campaign were never spelled out in legislation. Similarly, the nuclear waste program would evolve for thirty years without explicit legislative direction until the passage of the 1982 Nuclear Waste Policy Act.

But another similarity between nuclear policy and military installations policy is that these cozy arrangements were broken up in a variety of ways during the 1970s. The passage of the National Environmental Policy Act (NEPA) in 1969 and the Clean Air Act in 1970 provided new avenues to consumer groups and states to challenge federal dominance of nuclear policy (Jacob 1990, 32–33). In 1973, the Atomic Energy Commission was broken up into the Nuclear Regulatory Commission (NRC) and the Energy Research and Development Administration (ERDA), which would later become the Department of Energy (DOE) (Jacob 1990, 27). Finally, in 1977, Congress eliminated the Joint Atomic Energy Committee, splintering jurisdiction over nuclear-waste legislation among three Senate and seven House committees (*Congressional Quarterly* 1985, 364).

In total, these changes provided new tools for groups and states to challenge federal authority on nuclear policy, new points of access to challenge the nuclear industry's dominance of nuclear policy such as the widened number of congressional committees and the new legal tools available to groups seeking to sue in federal court, and new opportunities for political entrepreneurs in Congress to become part of the nuclear policy process. At the same time this was happening, and in part because the black box of nuclear policy had been opened up, the nuclear industry found itself on the negative end of the evening news more often than ever before. Gerald Jacob (1990, 57) argues,

> Reports of nuclear accidents became commonplace in the mass media; bizarre accidents attracted public attention. In 1975 a fire at the Browns Ferry, Alabama, reactor started by a technician checking for leaks with a candle, knocked out 15 percent of the electrical capacity on the TVA grid. The story was published in *Newsweek* magazine, and stories of "nuclear slapstick" became common. It became difficult to sustain a confidence in engineered solutions under such assaults. Nineteen seventy-nine was a very bad year for the nuclear establishment with Three Mile Island, the Kerr-McKee/Silkwood verdict, the release of the movie *China Syndrome*, and an antinuclear march on Washington attended by tens of thousands of people.

In addition to all the bad press, there was a more immediate problem building up. By 1982, eighty-two nuclear power plants were in operation in the United States and by 1980, these plants had already accumulated 25,000 spent fuel assemblies that they were storing "temporarily." Moreover, a DOE estimate in 1981 concluded that temporary storage capacity at reactor sites would no longer be adequate by 1986 (*Congressional Quarterly* 1985, 362).

Meanwhile, without direction from Congress, the ERDA, and later the DOE, had begun to attempt to address the problem of disposing of spent fuel. By 1977, attention was already focused on a limited number of sites that would remain the main contenders for a high-level nuclear waste facility over the next decade. Luther Carter (1987, 131–32) points out that in that year, Colin Heath, the director of geologic disposal for ERDA, prepared a memorandum that proposed limiting the siting search to six "salt states"—states that have geologic formations of either domed or bedded salt—and sites in Washington and Nevada. The Washington and Nevada sites offered special advantages, in part because of the specific geologic formations there—basalt in Washington and a variety of rock formations, including tuff, in Nevada. In addition, however, these sites were more politically palatable. Carter (1987, 132) points out that many governors and members of Congress had advised ERDA to look first to such government-owned reservations:

> That these federal reservations offered some significant advantages for repository siting was indeed apparent. They were located in remote desert regions; as special national security areas they were well policed; and they were already contaminated, at least in part, from the production of plutonium or the testing of nuclear weapons.

All this raises the question of why DOE did not simply march forward and unilaterally choose a site for the nation's high-level nuclear waste. There are several reasons. First, no state wanted to take the nation's commercial high-level nuclear waste and each state's congressional delegation was gearing up to keep such waste out. For this reason, if for no other, Congress was sure to weigh in on the issue. And as already pointed out, each of these congressional delegations now had new tools at their disposal. New forms of decision making in the field of nuclear policy had emerged as a result of sunshine laws, dispersal of authority to a greater number of committees in Congress, more staff, and the Freedom of Information Act. State and local authorities had developed significant expertise independent of federal decision makers, making it easier for them to challenge geologic and engineering claims made by DOE (Jacob 1990, 48–51). Additionally, opponents of any particular siting proposal were emboldened by what Jacob (1990, 47) calls "the emergence of a view of the priorities and functions of the state which emphasized environmental protection, public health, and safety" throughout the 1970s. Moreover, this movement had more than public opinion at its disposal. It had the legal tools provided by NEPA and the Clean Air Act. Finally, and perhaps most importantly, DOE could never have unilaterally made a decision about siting a high-level nuclear waste facility because any facility would require billions of dollars to study and construct—money that Congress would need to make available.

For all these reasons, then, Congress needed and wanted to deal with the problem of siting a high-level nuclear waste facility in the early 1980s. The task would not be easy, however. Choosing a site presents a collective-action problem similar to those already discussed in this study. Understanding the procedures Congress chose to deal with this problem requires, of course, that we first understand why it would be difficult for Congress to choose a site. It is to a description of that problem that we now turn.

The Problem Posed by Site Choice

Though we discussed above why Congress wanted and needed to design a process to choose a nuclear waste site, it is also rather easy to see why Congress would want to avoid the problem altogether. If legislators are, as Arnold asserts, concerned with negative policy effects of identifiable government actions that can then be traced back to their votes, we would expect that they would be especially leery of taking any traceable action that leads to the depositing of high-level nuclear waste in their state or district that will remain radioactive for tens of thousands of years. Much like base closure, then, the siting of a high-level nuclear waste facility necessarily involves a redistribution of the costs and benefits of nuclear energy that is particularly difficult for Congress, as an institution, to handle. The choice of a particular district can be expected to generate fierce opposition from the legislators in question as well as from legislators representing surrounding districts. Meanwhile, we would expect that the interest of the beneficiaries of such a decision—those who live near temporary storage sites for spent nuclear fuel—would be far less intense and enduring. This collective-action problem is commonly referred to as NIMBY (not-in-my-backyard).

A number of observers of the process of selecting a single national storage site for spent nuclear fuel have argued that this case does not conform well to the NIMBY syndrome. For instance, Gerald Jacob (1990, 42) cites evidence that local officials in Washington, Utah, Nevada, Colorado, and South Dakota expressed support for attempts to site the noxious facility in their towns. The lure of such a facility is not hard to imagine. In rural and depressed areas, the facility would provide good jobs with relatively high incomes.[3] These direct financial incentives were thus attractive to locals in comparison with the "intangible, vaguely defined, potential environmental impacts from a nuclear facility" (Jacob 1990, 43).

While such arguments have merit in explaining the behavior of some actors in intrastate politics, they do little to illuminate the dynamics surrounding the national legislature's attempts to choose a site for storage of spent nuclear fuel. Both Jacob and Carter acknowledge that despite local support for a facility at a few potential sites, this support was countered in each and every case by opposition from state governors and legislatures. Because the nuclear waste facility, in Jacob's (1990, 36) words, "lacked the pork barrel qualities or the status of a research center or reactor testing station like the Idaho National Engineering Lab," members of Congress were not fighting at the trough to land the facility in their district. Indeed, as we shall see, even after Congress included annual financial compensation for the host state of a permanent spent fuel storage facility, the congressional delegations of every state under consideration, including states explicitly highlighted by both Carter and Jacob as having locals supportive of hosting a facility, fought to keep the facility out. This observation is consistent with the economic model designed by Howard Kunreuther and Douglas Easterling, who conclude (1990, 255) that compensating local citizens in return for permission to site a hazardous facility is unlikely to have a positive effect on those who are already resistant, "unless the risk is perceived to be sufficiently low to oneself and to others, including future generations." They continue, this conclusion does not mean that tradeoffs between risk and benefits are inappropriate when it comes to siting hazardous facilities. Rather it suggests that before one attempts to initiate this process, some threshold of safety to nearby residents must be assured. (Kunreuther and Easterling 1990, 256)

In addition to the fact that compensation could not provide an easy out for Congress, there is another characteristic of the case of siting a spent fuel storage facility that made it a particularly difficult collective-action problem for Congress. In the case of base closure, the seeds of a coalition to close excess military bases always existed in the fact that not every congressional district has a major military base. Upon first glance, it might appear that similar seeds exist in choosing a site for storing the nation's commercial high-level nuclear waste. After all, as mentioned above, DOE had appeared to focus its efforts on six salt states plus Washington and Nevada. But, not surprisingly, the congressional delegations of those states had already worked hard to find ways to expand the possibilities. Some suggested that away-from-reactor (AFR) storage sites—located in South Carolina, New York, and Illinois—should take the spent fuel assemblies from reactors around the country. More significantly, others seized on the technological weaknesses of the argument for permanent geologic disposal to argue for a single storage facility where spent fuel assemblies could be temporarily stored, monitored, and later retrieved, once better technology was available. The facility came to be known as monitored, retrievable storage (MRS) and, significantly, the champion of this proposal was Senator J. Bennett Johnston (D-LA), an influential legislator from a prime salt state. As Jacob (1990, 76) points out, the beauty of MRS was that it "could be located virtually anywhere in the country since it did not depend upon local geology, such as Louisiana's salt domes, to isolate radioactive waste from the biosphere." Others wanted DOE to reexamine the possibility of siting a permanent geologic repository in granite—a move that would include most of the states in the Northeast in the search for a national repository. In short, in this atmosphere, though some were politically advantaged, virtually every state and congressional district could conceivably become the nation's home for spent nuclear fuel assemblies. The seeds of a coalition to choose a single national nuclear waste dump were thus not readily apparent.

Whodunnit? 1982 NWPA and the Amendments of 1987

The process by which a permanent national repository for spent nuclear fuel would be chosen was outlined in NWPA in 1982 and then amended by

Congress in 1987. As originally designed in NWPA, the process appears to delegate power to DOE to choose two national repository sites according to a strict timetable. Within 180 days of the act's enactment, DOE was required to develop guidelines that outline criteria for site selection. Shortly thereafter, DOE was required to recommend at least five candidate sites to the president for site characterization. Before January 1, 1985, DOE was required to narrow the list of candidate sites for characterization from five to three. Finally, on the basis of DOE site characterization of the three candidate sites, NWPA required the president to recommend a single site by March 31, 1987. The law also required the president to recommend a site for a second repository by March 31, 1990 and outlined a specific timetable leading up to that decision as well.

NWPA also appeared, on its surface, to provide numerous protections to state and local officials hostile to the siting of a nuclear waste repository within their borders. Before any site could be nominated by DOE to the president, the law required DOE to hold hearings in the vicinity of the site both to inform local residents and to receive comments. Environmental assessments prepared during DOE's search were required to be made public. Moreover, the law provided funds to states and localities seeking to assist them in reviewing the scientific work of DOE, developing requests for impact assistance, monitoring site characterization activities, and providing information to residents about site characterization. Most importantly, however, once a single site had been selected, the host state or, if applicable, Indian tribe would have the power to veto the federal decision. In addition to these protections, other provisions in NWPA required DOE to report on the feasibility of an MRS facility by June 1, 1985 and required NRC to issue a license for such a facility if Congress authorized its construction.

For all these reasons, then, the siting of the nation's high-level nuclear waste repository appears to have been handled by delegating power to technical experts. Specifically, the process appears to rule out meddling by members of Congress. Writing in 1987 of NWPA, then Governor and later U.S. Senator Richard Bryan (D-NV) (1987, 15) argued that lawmakers consciously attempted to craft a process that would designate a site scientifically and "keep political factors from taking over the site selection process."

Such an impression of the process is inaccurate, however. The process was not nearly as extra-congressional as it appeared. There are countless ways in which we can see that congressional fingerprints were all over the final choice from start to finish. First, while NWPA authorized DOE to develop guidelines within six months for the site selection process, other provisions in the law severely circumscribed the options open to DOE in developing those guidelines. For instance, NWPA stated that sites should not qualify if they are "(1) in a highly populated area, or (2) adjacent to an area 1 mile by 1 mile having a population of not less than 1,000 individuals" (42 USC 10132). Such language effectively ruled out large parts of the eastern seaboard. Moreover, NWPA stated at various points that DOE was required to "consider the various geologic media in which sites for repositories may be located and, to the extent practicable, to recommend sites in different geologic media" (42 USC 10132) This language was repeated in a section in the law authorizing DOE to carry out site characterization activities "beginning with the candidate sites that have been approved under section 112 *and are located in various geologic media*" (42 USC 10133, my emphasis). The choices are narrowed even further later on when DOE "is authorized to identify three or more sites, at least two of which shall be in different geologic media in the continental United States, and at least one of which shall be in media other than salt" (42 USC 10193).

The importance of the specification that the sites chosen for characterization should be in different geologic media is not readily apparent. But when we consider the existing inventory of potential sites DOE had been investigating and the additional specification that the first repository site should be in a relatively unpopulated area, DOE is left with numerous sites in salt formations, the basalt medium of the Washington site, and the various rock formations at the Nevada site. If these are the only options—and we are about to see further evidence of why they were—it is not hard to see how both the Yucca Mountain, Nevada and Hanford, Washington sites were two of the final three sites selected for characterization. Some two years after Yucca Mountain and Hanford were included in the final three by DOE, Governor Bryan (1987, 34, my emphasis) of Nevada argued,

> when evaluated in relation to the other eight preselected sites that DOE considered in its limited screening effort, Yucca Mountain would have rated very low on the list had the department not used a *self-imposed* requirement that the three top sites selected for characterization be in three different rock types. Since Yucca Mountain was the only tuff site and Hanford the only basalt site, and since all of the remaining sites were located in salt formations, both Hanford and Yucca Mountain were guaranteed to be selected among the top three.

In light of the provisions of NWPA highlighted above, however, there is very little that is "self-imposed" about the push to locate three sites in various geologic media. DOE was merely acting on Congress's explicit language.

This brings us to a second way in which Congress limited the search for a permanent geologic disposal site. Though NWPA authorized DOE to issue guidelines to determine the best site, it gave DOE 180 days to issue those guidelines. In the meantime, NWPA also required DOE to notify states "with one or more potentially acceptable sites for a repository within 90 days after the date of enactment" (42 USC 10136). Thus, DOE was required by law to identify "potentially acceptable sites" ninety days *before* issuing guidelines for its search. In effect, then, NWPA had given legal sanction to DOE siting efforts already underway. And those efforts were taking place in salt states such as Mississippi, Louisiana, Texas, and Utah, and at the basalt site in Washington and the tuff site in Nevada. DOE complied with this provision in February 1983, identifying nine sites and notifying the six states (Mississippi, Texas, and Utah each had two sites) in which they were located. Not surprisingly, Governor Bryan (1987, 16) viewed the decision with skepticism: "Rather than engaging in a truly national site-screening program aimed at finding the best site for a nuclear waste repository, DOE proceeded arbitrarily to focus on only nine sites, which had been under review before passage of NWPA."

When DOE finally issued its siting guidelines about eighteen months behind schedule in December 1984, it viewed the guidelines as criteria by which to narrow the list from nine sites to three. DOE did not believe, however, that Congress wanted the department to reconsider its initial decision on "potentially acceptable sites." A GAO (1985, 20) report to Congress indicated,

> Despite criticism from some of the affected states, DOE does not plan to reconsider its initial identification of the nine sites using the final siting guidelines. According to DOE's May 1983 response to comments on the proposed siting guidelines, the Congress did not intend for the initial site selections to be reconsidered using the final guidelines because the act (sec. 116(a)) required DOE to identify states containing "potentially acceptable sites" within 90 days of the act's passage, but allowed 180 days for issuing the siting guidelines. Consequently, DOE believes the site identification required by the act would have been impossible if the Congress had intended that DOE use the final siting guidelines to select sites for the first repository. DOE officials told us that a reconsideration of all possible sites would (1) require two or three years to complete and (2) probably result in selecting the same sites. DOE plans to carry out the remaining siting activities for the first repository and all screening activities for the second repository in accordance with the final siting guidelines.

To this explanation, Bryan (1987, 16) responded by arguing, "it is incomprehensible that Congress would have enacted NWPA—let alone included language explicitly critical of prior DOE efforts—had it intended for the department to merely continue ongoing site selection activities."

Most observers disagree with Bryan's interpretation, however. Indeed, it was because DOE could not move forward with its siting efforts on its own that Congress gave those efforts legal sanction. Gerald Jacob (1990, xv) points out that throughout the congressional debate over NWPA, "the states that would host deep geologic repositories were already known. There were few doubts about the outcome of the post-NWPA site selection process." Jacob (1990, 11) also points out, "NWPA was not a break with the past; it set no new administrative gears in motion but merely confirmed existing powers, priorities, and practices."

Thus, while Bryan viewed NWPA as an attempt by Congress to stop DOE from deviating from a scientific site-selection process, a more accurate interpretation would be that Congress was attempting to help DOE move along the selection process already underway. Realizing that DOE would need funds for site-characterization activities and construction of a repository and legal sanction for putting the nation's commercial nuclear waste in one place, Congress enacted NWPA, including provisions meant to direct DOE to a politically feasible choice in site selection.

This interpretation of NWPA leads us to a third way in which Congress limited the search DOE would conduct. It was pointed out earlier that states were given the right to disapprove a decision by DOE to site the repository within their borders. It is hard to imagine any state not exercising such a veto and this could conceivably open up the search anew. There are, however, two important provisions of NWPA, not yet discussed, that were designed to prevent this from happening. First, NWPA gave Congress the power to override a state's veto simply by passing a resolution in both houses. While this action is conceivably a high hurdle, legislators would be voting on such a resolution with the knowledge that reopening the process could put their own state in harm's way. The logic of such a vote would thus be that the only members of Congress likely to vote to sustain the state's veto would be those from the host state. Moreover, the act required that congressional consideration of the state's notice of disapproval be guided by NRC data—the same source that would have produced DOE's recommendation (Jacob 1990, 126). In effect, therefore, the state power to veto DOE's siting decision was of little use. Second, NWPA created a nuclear waste fund into which consumers of nuclear power would pay user fees. This fund would then be used for site characterization and repository construction activities, freeing Congress from the need to appropriate money for these purposes. The importance of this provision extends far beyond the realm of accounting, however. The appropriations process could have provided a loophole useful to legislators from a host state seeking to block construction of a repository. It would not be hard to imagine a senator from a host state filibustering an appropriations bill or a well-placed member of the House blocking an appropriations bill that includes funds for the construction of a repository. The nuclear waste fund helps Congress to avoid these obstacles.[4]

It is clear, then, that in enacting NWPA, Congress intended to provide DOE with legal sanction to go ahead with siting activities already underway. And since the primary potential targets of that effort were already known and the vast majority of legislators' districts were not in the cross hairs, and because the MRS provisions held out hope even for those states that were, NWPA was enacted by a bipartisan majority in both houses.[5] But while congressional control of the site selection process was subtle and quiet in NWPA, it was forceful and loud in the amendments to NWPA passed in 1987.

The 1987 amendments can be viewed as an attempt by the Congress to clean up the work done in NWPA. As argued above, Congress knew full well in passing NWPA what path DOE would take in implementing the law. By 1986, DOE had recommended a site in Deaf Smith, Texas, the Hanford, Washington site, and the Yucca Mountain, Nevada site for site characterization, thus narrowing the list from nine to three. In addition, DOE had also begun to focus on its Oak Ridge, Tennessee facility as a potential home for an MRS facility. It was at this point that Congress would take any semblance of discretion in the matter away from DOE and unilaterally choose Yucca Mountain as the sole site for the nation's geologic repository.

The 1987 amendments to NWPA required DOE to suspend all research and site characterization activities at all sites other than Yucca Mountain. Provisions in the law stipulated that if DOE found Yucca Mountain to be an unsuitable site for the nation's permanent geologic repository, the department should come back to Congress for further instruction. Looking back on the 1987 law, Senator Larry Craig (R-ID) admitted, "we did arbitrarily reach out and pick Yucca Mountain, no question about that."[6] Numerous unsuccessful appeals to the courts and the Congress by Nevada over the past two decades have delayed DOE's work at Yucca Mountain, but they have not come close to stopping it. NWPA required that the federal government take possession of the spent nuclear fuel being stored around the country in 1998—the time when Congress assumed a national repository would be ready. But by 1998, DOE had not yet completed its site characterization and licensing activities at Yucca Mountain. As a result, many in Congress sought to "temporarily" move the nation's commercial waste to Yucca Mountain and store it there until the repository was approved and ready. During that debate, Representative John Ensign (R-NV) (1998, 25) summed up what he viewed as the logic behind NWPA, the 1987 amendments, and everything that had happened since:

> Congress has decided this issue, not the scientists. What Congress is doing in [the 1998] bill is saying, with Yucca Mountain and the temporary storage site at the Nevada test site, "I do not care what any of the scientists say. It is going to be the site, and it is going to be suitable, and we are going to lower the standards until it is suitable."

The 1987 amendments also took other steps to ensure that all the nation's spent nuclear fuel would go to Yucca Mountain. First, it nullified DOE's proposal to site an MRS facility in Oak Ridge, Tennessee and required that in searching for a site for an MRS facility, DOE "shall make no presumption or preference to such sites by reason of their previous selection" (42 USC 10162). Not only was DOE supposed to start over on MRS, a provision was added prohibiting DOE from selecting a site until after a permanent repository had gone through site characterization and been approved (42 USC 10165). Congress would still need to appropriate funds for such a facility, however, and if the permanent repository was ready for construction, there would be little incentive to begin construction of an MRS facility. The philosophical idea behind MRS was to put the spent fuel someplace where it could be monitored and then retrieved once the technology was available for permanent storage. In effect, then, the provision delaying site selection for MRS until after Yucca Mountain was approved was a provision to kill MRS.

Similarly, the 1987 amendments also contained provisions designed to block the search for a second repository. In contrast with the provisions of NWPA that called for DOE to recommend a site for a second permanent repository by 1990, the 1987 law stated, "the Secretary shall report to the President and to Congress on or after January 1, 2007, but not later than January 1, 2010, on the need for a second repository" (42 USC 10172a). Even this report is unlikely to emerge, however, because the law also stated that DOE "may not conduct site-specific activities with respect to a second repository unless Congress has specifically authorized and appropriated funds for such activities" (42 USC 10172a). Moreover, the new law required DOE to phase out all activities "designed to evaluate the suitability of crystalline rock as a potential repository host medium" (42 USC 10172a). The purpose of this provision was to rule out granite as a host medium, thus taking most of the East Coast out of consideration as a host for a second repository.

As if the point that Yucca Mountain was the only show in town had not been hammered home clearly enough, the 1987 law also conditioned compensatory payments to the host state on that state's decision to waive its veto rights under NWPA. The law discusses in some detail how and when a state will be compensated, offering $10 million per year to the state once a construction license is approved and $20 million per year once the facility is built and receiving spent fuel. But later, the law requires that any benefits agreement provide that "the State or Indian tribe that is party to such agreement waive its right under title I to disapprove the recommendation of a site for a repository" (42 USC 10173a). With this provision, the veto rights guaranteed in NWPA take on even less meaning.[7]

We have seen, then, that it was Congress, and really Congress alone, that decided to put the nation's commercial spent nuclear fuel in Yucca Mountain. This point is central to the question that guides this study. When conferring general benefits and imposing particularistic costs, why does Congress sometimes delegate power utilizing extra-congressional procedures and, in other cases, enact these policies internally? The point we have made is that, all appearances aside in this case, Congress was responsible for choosing Yucca Mountain from start to finish. We have seen how NWPA and the 1987 amendments to NWPA focused the particularistic costs on Yucca Mountain. Writing in 1990, Gerald Jacob (1990, xviii) asks, "Was the outcome ever in doubt? The evidence suggests the answer must be 'rarely.'" The next question is how Congress was able to pass these laws on its own.

Procedures as Key

In discussing how Congress forced the nation's commercial spent nuclear fuel on Nevada, Douglas Arnold (1990, 111–12) remarks, "this solution, which seems so obvious to armchair theorists, required nearly a decade for Congress to accept. Concentrating costs on the tiniest group or area is seldom the easiest way to build a coalition in Congress."

This statement serves as an excellent reminder that designating Yucca Mountain as the nation's sole repository for spent fuel required more than simple math (531 other members of Congress versus 4 from Nevada). It required the deft use of procedures.

The critical procedural maneuver in the passage of NWPA was the adoption of a closed rule in the House. Throughout the legislative process leading up to the enactment of NWPA, various members of Congress had attempted to amend the legislation to explicitly preclude selection of a site in their district or state. Coalition leaders from both houses were also seeking to avoid having to go to conference on the legislation as that would provide further openings for legislators seeking to protect their districts and states. Finally, legislators needed to avoid a conference as the ninety-seventh Congress was winding down and not enough time remained. The state veto provision in NWPA was only as strong as it was because Senator William Proxmire (D-WI) had threatened to filibuster the bill without it. The amendment to satisfy Proxmire and the bill itself were finally agreed to by the Senate on December 20, 1982, leaving no time for a conference.

To avoid all these problems, just a few hours after the Senate had completed its work on NWPA, the House voted on a rule for consideration of the Senate version that provided for no amendments and, more importantly, provided that the vote to adopt the rule was also the vote to pass the bill (*Congressional Quarterly* 1985, 365–66). The importance of this procedure cannot be overstated. The closed rule forced legislators to weigh the general benefit it was likely to deliver versus what was, for most legislators, the incredibly unlikely possibility that the process NWPA called for would put a high-level nuclear waste repository in their district. In this light, the rule was adopted and the bill was enacted by a vote of 256–32.

Procedural tactics played an even larger role in the passage of the 1987 amendments to NWPA. One important difference between 1982 and 1987 was that by 1987, Democrats had regained control of the Senate and the new chairman of the Senate Energy Committee was J. Bennett Johnston (D-LA). As a minority member of the committee in 1982, Johnston had been the main proponent of including provisions in NWPA that allowed DOE to move forward with research and siting of an MRS facility—a move designed to provide an alternative to a permanent geologic repository which had a chance of being located in Louisiana (*Congressional Quarterly* 1985, 364). With the list of potential geologic repository sites narrowed down to Deaf Smith, TX, Hanford, WA, and Yucca Mountain, NV in 1987, Johnston became the primary architect of what has come to be known among critics as the "screw Nevada bill"—the 1987 amendments to NWPA. While Arnold (1990, 111) argues that with the search narrowed to Texas, Washington, and Nevada, "coalition leaders finally had the nucleus for an unbeatable coalition," the truth is that the next step would still be difficult. As Arnold himself pointed out earlier, ganging up on tiny Nevada, or any state no matter how weak, remains difficult both because of congressional norms and, perhaps more importantly, because of the danger of a filibuster.

The fiscal 1988 reconciliation bill provided the procedural vehicle Johnston needed. As originally crafted by Johnston, the amendments to

NWPA would require DOE to engage in site-characterization activities at only one of the three sites the department had on its list, though Johnston's bill left the choice up to DOE. The rationale, at least publicly, for attaching the plan to the reconciliation bill was that conducting one site characterization instead of three would save $634 million over three years—most of the $730 million in savings over three years Johnston's Energy Committee was required to find to meet its reconciliation target (*Congressional Quarterly* 1990, 484).

Johnston's original plan also included provisions to authorize an MRS facility once a permanent facility was licensed. This provision was important because, as a backup, Johnston, who also served as the chairman of the Appropriations Subcommittee for Energy and Water Development, also attached his plan to the fiscal 1988 energy and water appropriations bill. The political logic of attaching the plan to the appropriations bill was that Johnston would then be able to go to conference on the bill with the chairman of the House Appropriations Committee, Representative Jamie Whitten (D-MS)—a member from a state, like Louisiana, that was among the six final states under consideration for a permanent geologic repository but not one of the final three. While this backup proved to be unnecessary, the maneuver highlighted the procedural importance of including the plan as part of the reconciliation bill. Fellow members of the Appropriations Subcommittee for Energy and Water Development, Senators Harry Reid (D-NV) and Jim Sasser (D-TN) attempted to eliminate Johnston's plan from the appropriations bill (*Congressional Quarterly* 1990, 484). Reid was seeking to keep the permanent facility out of Nevada and Sasser was attempting to keep an MRS facility out of Tennessee. These junior members of the committee failed to keep Johnston's plan off the appropriations bill, but Reid, along with Senator Brock Adams (D-WA), whose state also remained in the cross hairs for the permanent facility, made good on a threat to filibuster the bill on the floor—a tactic that kept the bill off the floor for several weeks (*Congressional Quarterly* 1990, 485). The demonstration made clear that Nevada would not give up without a fight. But it made something else clear as well—the difference in procedural advantages between reconciliation bills and appropriations bills. Reconciliation bills cannot be filibustered. Seeing the writing on the wall, Sasser cut a separate deal with Johnston. An amendment added a provision that would delay MRS while it was being studied by a blue-ribbon commission (*Congressional Quarterly* 1990, 485–86). Tennessee was off the hook.

Not surprisingly, Johnston opted to let the reconciliation conference have first crack at his plan. A House bill on nuclear waste approved by

Representative Morris Udall's (D-AZ) Interior Committee had gone in almost a completely opposite direction from Johnston's plan. Udall's bill called for a bipartisan commission from within the legislative branch to study DOE's handling of the waste issue, review the foundation of NWPA, and report back to Congress on what legislation would be needed. During this period, DOE would be prohibited from further studying sites for a permanent repository (*Congressional Quarterly* 1990, 486).

Nevertheless, when the conference convened, the political logic of the situation became overwhelming. None of Nevada's four members of Congress were involved. Texas and Washington, on the other hand, each had strong representation in conference. The Texas representatives demanded a provision that DOE could not choose as a site for characterization any site that lay below an aquifer—an underground stream. The Texas and Washington sites both lay below an aquifer and the Nevada site did not. Johnston agreed and conferees later agreed to drop the murky provision on an aquifer and simply name Nevada as the sole site. Along the way, House conferees, in a nod to fellow conferee Representative Jim Cooper (D-TN), convinced Johnston to make authorization of an MRS facility conditional on DOE first approving Yucca Mountain as the nation's permanent geologic repository (*Congressional Quarterly* 1990, 487). In the end, then, a conference seeking to negotiate between Johnston's plan to speed up the selection process and Udall's plan to slow it down had sped the process up even more than Johnston had originally imagined.

Members' comments before the vote to approve the conference report on the reconciliation bill highlight the importance of Johnston's procedural maneuver. Not only did the procedural tactic preclude amendments and filibusters, it also packaged the plan with a massive reconciliation bill promising $76 billion in deficit reduction over two years. Legislators thinking about voting against the package would thus have to justify not only why they voted against moving nuclear waste out of their constituents' backyards, but also why they voted against reducing the deficit. Moreover, because the hardest pills to swallow in the bill were hammered out in conference, Johnston was quick to blame them on the House conferees—a group that had come into conference seeking to delay the site-selection process. Johnston pointed out that "the House conferees insisted on the selection of the Nevada site by Congress"[8] and "the amount of money available to a host State was reduced substantially in the conference agreement at the insistence of the House conferees."[9]

Regardless of who was to blame, however, members found themselves with a clear choice. Representative Udall argued, "the procedural course adopted by the other body is regrettable"[10] and suggested that he doubts "any one will point to this bill as a noble example of our democratic system's ability to resolve sensitive technical issues."[11] In the end, however, he supported the conference report. Representative Philip Sharp (D-IN) complained that "the expedited procedures of the Reconciliation Act should not have been used for this important matter," but added, "it has the virtue of cutting through the pretense under some legislative proposals that any genuine consideration of other sites would occur."[12] Highlighting the importance of Johnston's procedural maneuver, Representative Douglas Owens (D-UT) pointed out that designating Nevada as the sole national site for a geologic repository would bring tons of nuclear waste through his state. Nevertheless, he concluded,

> I will vote to accept the conference report, which makes Utah a victim with Nevada and "the crossroads of the waste," only because we must, above all legislative imperatives, reduce the budget deficit. If we were permitted a separate vote on the nuclear waste provision of this bill, I would vote "Hell No."[13]

Representative Cooper of Tennessee, of course, also supported the conference report "reluctantly"; thanked those who had been responsible for including him in the conference committee; and expressed his heartfelt, though unsatisfied, desire to help Nevada.

> My primary concern during the conference was defeating the Department of Energy's ill-conceived plans to locate a monitored retrievable storage (MRS) facility near Oak Ridge, TN. But my concern was not the selfish one of wishing the nuclear waste on someone else.[14]

At the same time, of course, those from Nevada cried foul. Representative Barbara Vucanovich (R-NV) argued that the bill would "turn our state into a federal colony" and declared, "Congress is behaving like a pack of wolves going in for the kill."[15] Vucanovich and Senator Reid also complained that nobody from Nevada had been appointed to the conference committee, with Reid declaring that Nevada had been "shut out completely."[16] Johnston responded, "they weren't shut out. They just weren't appointed to the conference."[17] Reid also took to the floor with language strong enough for the Civil War:

> It is with a sense of revulsion and shame that I rise today to speak on the budget reconciliation legislation that shortly will be before us; revulsion

at what can only be described as oppression and colonialism, directed at
the people of my State by forty-nine other States who are supposed to be
our allies in a political union; shame because the sad truth is that this legislation has been subverted into becoming a vehicle for the grossest kind
of political chicanery.[18]

Inflammatory language aside, however, what is clear from the legislative history of NWPA and the 1987 amendments to NWPA is that procedural tactics—the use of closed rules, omnibus legislative vehicles, legislating in conference, and the use of special reconciliation procedures—were central to the
congressional effort to designate Nevada as the sole site for the nation's commercial spent nuclear fuel.

Applying the Theory:
Procedural Choice and Nuclear Waste Disposal

That procedures were central to the congressional selection of Yucca
Mountain is thus clear. What is less clear is *why* coalition leaders chose the
procedural path they did. More specifically, why did legislators choose to
impose a geographically concentrated particularistic cost utilizing internal
procedures in this case while utilizing extra-congressional procedures in the
case of base closure? Answering this question requires that we turn our attention to the five propositions we have been examining throughout this study.
What we find in examining those propositions is that while most of the political dynamics of siting a high-level nuclear waste facility are similar to the
political dynamics of base closure, there are a very few differences in the
nature of the particularistic cost that account for its different procedural
treatment.

Proposition I. Geographic Concentration of Costs

Despite the claim of some observers that the siting of a high-level nuclear
waste facility does not conform well to the NIMBY syndrome, there is no
shortage of evidence to demonstrate that the geographic cost being imposed
was more sensitive than the average particularistic cost. The language utilized
by Senator Reid above is but one example of the desperation legislators felt
in attempting to keep the spent nuclear fuel out of their districts. During congressional deliberation over NWPA, virtually every state maneuvered to keep
the site outside their borders. States west of the Mississippi attempted, but

failed, to amend the law to prohibit nuclear waste from being transported more than five hundred miles from where it was generated—a provision designed to keep the waste in the East where more nuclear reactors were located (Jacob 1990, 123). Eastern states argued for a remote, permanent facility with the emphasis on *remote* (Jacob 1990, 41). In 1987, the dispute became even more heated and the comments of members even more explicit. Senator George Mitchell (D-ME) expressed how "pleased" he was with the outcome, because the new language in the reconciliation bill meant that "DOE is not authorized to conduct any activities related to a second site and DOE can no longer consider Maine as a potential nuclear waste site."[19] Representative Al Swift (D-WA), who had been instrumental in guaranteeing that Washington would get off the hook along with Texas, described what had happened in conference as "a goddamned outrage," but also made clear what his priority had been: "If we are going to have to do it over a barrel, then this configuration gives me the parochial things that I need" (*Congressional Quarterly* 1990, 487). He would add, "we are going to give somebody some nasty stuff" (*Congressional Quarterly* 1990, 483). As we saw earlier, Representative Cooper had jumped on board the 1987 band-wagon when conferees assured him provisions would be added delaying con-struction of an MRS facility. Expressing sympathy for Nevada at the time, Cooper claimed his victory was "bittersweet." What he should have said instead was that his victory was "incomplete" because just a few years later, with the House Energy and Commerce Committee working on a bill to speed up the licensing process for the permanent facility in Nevada, Cooper had insisted not only on maintaining the prohibition on licensing an MRS facili-ty until after a permanent facility had been licensed but also on a provision that ordered DOE to locate the MRS facility "as close as possible" to the Yucca Mountain site (Idelson 1991b, 2613).

One other measure of the particular sensitivity of this geographic cost is the electoral cost. Though Senator Chic Hecht (R-NV) did oppose the 1987 amendments to NWPA, arguing that the waste should be reprocessed instead of buried, most observers agree that he subsequently lost his reelection bid in 1988 because he did not oppose the plan actively enough. Though Hecht him-self claimed to have made the bill much better by adding amendments along the way,[20] it is worth mentioning that he received no thanks from any of the three other members of the Nevada congressional delegation. Note, for instance, Hecht's absence from Representative James Bilbray's (D-NV) comments: "Our delegation has fought together. The gentlewoman from Nevada [Mrs. Vucanovich] and myself and the junior Senator from our State have fought vigorously to oppose this."[21]

Later Bilbray added,

> Nevada's House delegation has fought shoulder to shoulder to bring sense to this body. My friend and colleague, Congresswoman Barbara Vucanovich, has worked long and hard to keep nuclear waste out of Nevada. In the other body, Senator Harry Reid led a long filibuster to try to prevent what is happening here today.[22]

Not surprisingly, a common refrain heard in the wake of Hecht's 1988 reelection loss to Governor Richard Bryan was that Hecht was not opposed *enough* to the dump. For instance, *Congressional Quarterly* (Idelson 1992, 3142) reported that Hecht had lost,

> largely on the basis of [his] belated opposition to the planned Yucca dump. And Hecht's malapropism—he once said he did not want the state to become "a nuclear suppository"—did little to persuade Nevadans of the seriousness with which he approached the issue.

Thus, there is no question that because siting this nuclear waste facility in a particular place imposes geographically concentrated costs, it was far more sensitive and far more important to legislators to avoid blame than would have been the case if the costs were particularistic but geographically dispersed. But there is reason to believe that this type of geographic cost is, in fact, even more difficult to swallow than the geographic costs imposed by base closure. Legislators seek to keep bases open because they believe constituents working in and around these bases will face heavy economic losses if the base is closed and will seek to punish the legislator in the next election. We saw earlier that Kunreuther and Easterling found that citizens will be unwilling to accept the presence of a hazardous waste facility in their district in exchange for compensation unless they have reason to believe the physical harm to them and to future generations will be minimal. But in addition to these costs, legislators seeking to keep a nuclear waste facility out of their district also have the same economic concerns as those working to keep a base open in their district. While legislators in Nevada worry about the impact on tourism in Las Vegas—a mere ninety miles from Yucca Mountain—the economic concerns of legislators elsewhere are no less frightening. For example, Representative Kent Hance (D-TX), who represented the district that contained the Deaf Smith site, received a letter from Frito-Lay—a company that purchased up to $23 million a year worth of corn and potatoes from the area in and around Hance's district—that contained the following passage:

> We all know that nuclear waste is an emotional issue, and it doesn't take much imagination to conjure up the eventual hue and cry of the public about food crops being irrigated by water that flows over nuclear waste. Under such a situation our alternative would be to move into other corn and potato producing areas for raw materials, seriously disrupting the economy of your district. It seems that a far better alternative for every party concerned would be to locate nuclear waste disposals in areas of federally owned wastelands where even sage brush has a hard time growing.[23]

The dual dimensions of the geographic cost—both environmental and economic—imply a theoretical explanation for what we have seen above. Legislators have even more reason to be concerned with a nuclear waste facility being located in their district than they do with losing a military base.

So why didn't legislators delegate? One part of the answer to this question that deserves mention is that legislative leaders did consciously attempt to mitigate some of the costs borne by the host community. As mentioned earlier, a compensation package was included that was to deliver $10 million per year to Nevada once the site was licensed and $20 million per year once the site began accepting spent fuel.[24] In addition, Nevada was also given assurances in 1987 that it would receive special consideration for other federal projects such as the Superconducting Super-Collider Project (Jacob 1990, 170–71)—a promise that yielded no fruit. Finally, whether intentionally or not, legislators did choose a site that was least likely to provoke local resistance. Yucca Mountain is located on federal land that served in the past as a nuclear test site that is already considered to be contaminated. Moreover, the surrounding area is rural and poor—a demography less likely to be resistant to the jobs and federal dollars that will accompany the waste facility.

These geographic benefits that flow to Nevada from DOE activities notwithstanding, the geographic concentration of costs offers more questions than answers when it comes to procedural choice. The proposition related to geography suggests that members of Congress should want to delegate this decision, if not to the DOE or some other standing agency, then to an ad hoc commission empowered to make the decision. The puzzle becomes all the more confusing when we recall that various proposals to do just that were considered and rejected at a number of points in the process.[25]

Proposition II. Scope of the Policy Area

We expect legislators to be less willing to delegate power in policy areas that are broad and that allow greater discretion to decision makers. The task of finding a national site to house only one type of hazardous waste is a some-what narrow policy problem; therefore, we might expect that Congress would be willing to delegate authority without fear that delegation would spill over into other policy areas. Furthermore, because members of Congress had very little trust in DOE[26]—this is similar to members' lack of trust in the Pentagon in base closure—we might expect Congress to delegate to an ad hoc commission to site a facility instead. Nevertheless, as we have seen, Congress did not choose to delegate authority in this policy area.

That said, there is one point in the battle over siting a high-level nuclear waste facility that is relevant to this proposition and thus worth mentioning. One part of the reason Congress took so long to enact NWPA was that members disagreed over whether high-level nuclear waste from military programs ought to be stored in the same facility with high-level nuclear waste from commercial nuclear reactors (*Congressional Quarterly* 1985, 361). The issue was difficult, in part, because of the turf battles that commonly ensue when a legislative initiative cuts across the jurisdictional lines of standing congressional committees. But it was also difficult because including military waste in the facility would broaden the scope of the policy area. President Carter had issued an executive order prohibiting DOE from reprocessing spent nuclear fuel and using the byproducts to build nuclear weapons, but President Reagan had reversed that decision. While no spent fuel was reprocessed in the early 1980s, the Congress still decided to explicitly prohibit the federal government from reprocessing in 1982. This action is relevant within the context of nuclear waste disposal because it is an indicator of Congress's intent in keeping military and civilian nuclear programs separate and, by extension, keeping the scope of the policy area in siting a high-level nuclear waste facility narrow. Luther Carter (1987, 195) makes precisely this argument: "It should be pointed out that for most members of Congress the waste issue was strictly a domestic concern." Indeed, Senate Armed Services Chairman John Tower (R-TX) warned members that he would demand NWPA be referred to his committee if it included provisions to store military as well as civilian waste (*Congressional Quarterly* 1985, 364).

Surprisingly, in the end, NWPA effectively delegated authority to decide whether military waste should be stored with civilian waste to the president (42 USC 10107). While this chapter is primarily concerned with spent fuel from commercial nuclear reactors, it is worth noting that this provision is consistent with the proposition under discussion here. We might surmise that members of Congress felt comfortable delegating authority to the president to handle the military waste disposal question in part because they had peeled off a relatively small and narrow chunk of the policy area to be delegated.

Coming back to civilian nuclear waste, however, the relevant point for our purposes is that Congress chose not to delegate authority to site a high-level nuclear waste facility despite the fact that the policy area in question was sufficiently narrow. What this may suggest about this second proposition is that a narrow policy area is a necessary pre-condition for delegation, but it is not necessarily determinative. In other words, the scope of the policy area does not provide any positive incentive to delegate, but it can serve—in the case of a broad policy area—as a prohibitive factor. The reasons for *this* procedural choice, as we are about to see, were more a result of the moment in political time, the existence of powerful champions, and the number of geographic locations targeted than the geographic concentration of the cost imposed or the scope of the policy area.

Proposition III. Political Time

The particular moment in political time made it more likely legislators would handle the siting of a high-level nuclear waste facility internally rather than delegate it. As with any case in which legislators are seeking to impose particularistic costs in favor of a general benefit, legislative leaders were very sensitive to the electoral calendar and found ways to mitigate negative electoral impacts for most legislators. As Gerald Jacob (1990, 97) points out, NWPA "only materialized in the final, hectic hours of the Ninety-seventh Congress." Remember that in the case of base closure, coalition leaders had arranged for legislators to be able to vote for the notion of base closure in general just before the 1988 election, with the specific list of closures to be announced just after the election. Similarly, in the case of nuclear waste disposal, coalition leaders scheduled a vote at a point on the electoral calendar that left at least two full years (the siting process set in motion would take even longer) to get out from under the negative policy effects of their votes. This sensitivity to the electoral calendar also displayed itself in the struggle over the 1987 amendments to NWPA. After Senator Sasser of Tennessee had fought alongside Senator Reid to stop Johnston's bill in the appropriations committee, Johnston struck a deal with Sasser that would set up a commission to study whether MRS (the facility Sasser worried would be located in Tennessee) was feasible and, importantly, the commission was not expected to report back until January 1989—a scant two months after Sasser's expected reelection to the Senate.

But a second, and far more important, way in which the electoral calendar offered opportunities for coalition leaders to handle site selection internally has to do with the strength of Nevada's congressional delegation. Nevada's delegation is small and that, as we will discuss in a later section, was a critical factor. But in addition, the delegation was particularly weak in 1987. When the choice came down to Nevada, Washington, and Texas, there was no match, not only because of the relative sizes of the congressional delegations, but because of the institutional positions their members held. Douglas Arnold (1990, 112 n73) points out,

> In 1987 Senator Paul Laxalt (R.-Nev.), perhaps the president's closest friend in Congress, had just retired, and Nevada's four remaining legislators held no important positions and had virtually no seniority (two were elected in 1982, and two in 1986). Texas and Washington not only had size, committee positions, and seniority on their side, they were also the home states of Speaker Jim Wright and House Majority Leader Thomas Foley.

The same logic worked in reverse in 1998 when Nevada's delegation was much stronger. When most in Congress wanted to create a temporary waste site next to Yucca Mountain to store the spent fuel until the permanent site was constructed, Nevada found it had friends in high places. Challenging Senator Reid for his seat that year, Representative John Ensign (R-NV) was able to convince the Speaker of the House, Representative Newt Gingrich (R-GA), to keep the bill off the legislative calendar. At the same time, Senators Reid and Bryan killed the bill in the Senate by holding all but three Democrats with them on a cloture vote (McCutcheon 1998, 1536).

Proposition IV. Existence of Powerful Champions

In order for Congress to impose geographically concentrated costs using an internal legislative procedure, there must be some well-placed champion (or set of champions) willing to see the legislative vehicle over and through the many hurdles it is likely to encounter. In 1987, Johnston served as the chair of both the Senate Energy and Natural Resources Committee and the Appropriations Subcommittee on Energy and Water Development. Johnston certainly had a motive for seeing the nuclear waste issue resolved because Louisiana had been one of nine sites under consideration by DOE for a national permanent geologic disposal facility. More important than the motive, however, Johnston's institutional position provided him with the means. As we saw earlier, Johnston attached his plan (designed to single out Nevada) to both the Energy and Water Appropriations bill and to the fiscal 1988 reconciliation bill that ultimately was enacted. As a key player in the reconciliation conference, Johnston was able to cut deals when necessary[27] and present the final bill to the Senate as a fait accompli.[28]

The flip side of the proposition is worthy of note as well. While Johnston was utilizing his institutional position to get his way, his opponents found themselves with few institutional legs on which to stand. As noted above, Nevada's congressional delegation was not only small, it lacked seniority and institutional strength. None of the members of the delegation served as a chair of a relevant committee and none was part of the conference committee that ultimately decided the matter. Repeating Johnston's words, "they weren't shut out. They just weren't appointed to the conference."[29]

Proposition V. The One, the Few, and the Many

Site selection for a high-level nuclear waste facility differs from base closure as a collective-action problem in at least one very significant way. In base closure, legislators seek to impose particularistic costs on a number of geographic areas at once. In choosing a site for a waste facility, on the other hand, legislators single out one location to shoulder the costs while the rest of the nation shares in the general benefit. Moreover, while many congressional districts—Representative Armey's is a notable example—had no military installations of significant size, most congressional districts theoretically had to fear the prospect of one of a geologic, MRS, or AFR facility being placed in the district and accepting all of the nation's spent nuclear fuel. The minority to be overcome was thus smaller in the case of nuclear waste site choice and the natural majority of districts seeking to dodge this bullet was therefore larger. While it is a truism that a determined minority in Congress is quite capable of blocking action on any given bill, it is also the case that not all minorities in Congress are created equally. Specifically, all other things being equal, small minorities—we saw above that the minority in question was not only small, but weak—are less capable of blocking action than large minorities and larger majorities are more capable of overwhelming minorities than smaller majorities. In short, the mathematics of site choice is different than that of base closure. While singling out one site still requires that legislators target an identifiable, particular legislator, the task is much easier if it becomes a process of ganging up on the weakest member of the herd.

Not surprisingly, this process was a very slow one. The best analogy is to imagine it as an extended game of musical chairs. Luther Carter (1987, 197) points out that as NWPA began to take focus in Congress, there were about a dozen states that still remained as potential sites for either the first permanent geologic facility or a temporary storage facility for the nation's spent fuel. In addition to the six states eventually named by DOE as "potentially acceptable" in 1983 (Nevada, Washington, Texas, Utah, Louisiana, and Mississippi), three states with good granite formations were attracting attention (Wisconsin, Michigan, and Minnesota) and three others were considered likely homes for an AFR (South Carolina, Illinois, and New York). Carter's description of these states as a bloc suggests why it took so long for Congress to narrow its choice down to Nevada: "The host states all wanted the waste legislation to give them a strong voice, but in a number of instances their interests could be divergent or conflicting" (Carter 1987, 197). The salt states all wanted to include the upper midwest states in DOE's considerations. New York, Illinois, and South Carolina wanted to make sure a permanent facility would be built somewhere soon. Nevada and Washington wanted to be certain that states had as much veto power as possible.

Thus, the enactment of NWPA, DOE's implementation of NWPA, and the enactment of the amendments to NWPA in 1987 can all be seen as a long process of eliminating players from the game, sometimes one by one, until only one site remained. As we have seen, this process took on a variety of forms. Members of Congress from Tennessee were brought on board very late in the process when provisions were added to delay and study MRS. Members from Texas and Washington only came on board when they demanded and received, in conference, a provision to name Nevada as the sole site for characterization. Representative Edward Markey (D-MA) (1998, 17) described the process this way.

> We passed another bill in 1987. What did we say? Well, the [Speaker] of the House then came from Texas. He said, "I don't want it in Texas." That was one of the sites. The Majority Leader came from Washington State. He said, "I don't want it in Washington State." It was out. The third State was the salt domes in Louisiana. The Chairman of the Committee on Energy came from Louisiana. He said, "I don't want it in Louisiana," and it was out. The fourth site was in North Carolina. North Carolina was out. The fifth site was the solid granite of New Hampshire, and Ronald Reagan and George Bush said, "That is out in 1988. We are not burying all the nuclear waste in America in New Hampshire." So we kept searching, playing this game of thermonuclear hearts, trying to stick the queen of spades with somebody. So we looked around, and what did we find? We found the State of Nevada—two congressmen, two senators. "You get all the nuclear waste. We are picking you."

Imposing a geographically concentrated cost on one location in favor of a benefit for everyone else is not easy. But when the electoral calendar allowed it, when Nevada's congressional delegation was at its weakest point, and when legislative leaders had the motive and the means, other legislators stuck Nevada with the queen of spades.

Conclusion

It might seem odd to suggest the case of nuclear waste disposal is an example of "doing the right thing." After all, the preceding narrative hardly paints a pleasant picture of disinterested representatives of the people working toward the public interest. Rather it is a story that, at times, seems only to be about parochially oriented leaders using brute legislative force to overcome a temporarily weak opposition. In addition, in the years since 1987, a number of independent scientists and environmental groups have raised serious concerns about the scientific feasibility and the merits of the Yucca Mountain Project. From this vantage point, one might argue that if this is "doing the right thing," we don't even want to imagine what "doing the *wrong* thing" would look like.

Several responses to these objections are in order. First, while it is an accepted truism that the legislative process is rarely elegant or even orderly, those appearances should not color our view of the outcomes. As Publius argues in *The Federalist Papers,* self-interest can, at least on occasion, serve the public good.[30] A second, and perhaps more complex, response is that leaving the decision to site a nuclear waste facility to the "experts" is one fraught with more peril and pitfalls than those experts would have one believe. Along the road to choosing Yucca Mountain as the nation's sole site for a permanent geologic repository for spent nuclear fuel, even many legislators complained that the scientists and technicians were being forced to yield to politicians. While he remains a harsh critic of how site choice was handled in this case, Gerald Jacob (1990) argues that such complaints are misguided for two reasons. First, categorizing a decision as "technical" is often a simple way of shifting responsibility for making social and economic choices to others who may be less responsible to the electorate. But they do not eliminate the underlying value conflicts associated with those choices. Jacob (1990, 124) provides the following example:

> Determining what kind of bolt to use seems to be a straightforward, mundane technical decision best left to the engineer. However, the choice between a cost-saving, less durable bolt and a high-tolerance, but expensive one can affect the potential for catastrophic failure of a hotel skyway

or a nuclear power plant cooling system. Therefore, even this simple "technical" decision carries political implications: the specific geographic area and population exposed to a level of risk; the distribution of impacts and benefits associated with use of the cost-saving bolt instead of the more expensive one; and the social burden of responding to a catastrophe and treating its effects. Industry benefits from choosing the cost-saving bolt; however, the increased risk of injury or death is socialized. That is, the cost is distributed among the population at large. Complex decisions, such as which waste disposal technology or site to use, carry correspondingly complex and extensive political-economic implications.

A second reason Jacob (1990, 125) believes relegating decisions to technocrats in the case of a high-level nuclear waste site choice is misguided is that in this case, "unlike the question of how to rebuild an automobile carburetor, consensus cannot necessarily be reached on the basis of existing technical standards or practice." Because of this uncertainty, technical debates become proxies for debates about underlying value conflicts that go unresolved. For instance, it is not terribly surprising to imagine how Senator Johnston became such an ardent advocate of developing MRS technologies, while legislators from Tennessee had determined that permanent geologic disposal was a far better technical solution than MRS. Jacob's critique of technocratic alternatives to the process utilized for choosing a high-level nuclear waste facility thus offers a lesson to those who suggest that the choice of Yucca Mountain was arbitrary and merely about Goliath beating up on David. Waste was—and still is—piling up at "temporary" locations around the country. This is both an environmental and a national security risk not to be taken lightly in the post-9/11 world. Is Yucca Mountain the "right" place for nuclear waste? Scientists offer divergent viewpoints. In the worst light, the procedure utilized yielded a decision no more arbitrary than might have otherwise been the case. In a more positive light, the procedure did yield a decision and accountable elected officials in a Congress often criticized for failing to act, acted here.

Luther Carter (1987) suggests another lesson to be drawn from this site selection process. Writing before the 1987 amendments to NWPA were enacted, Carter argued that NWPA had delegated *too much* discretion to DOE. He suggests that in tackling similar policy problems in the future, legislators would be wise,

> to keep the geographic scope and procedural complexities of the site search within modest limits. To seek a distribution of potential repository sites over several regions is more likely to spread the misery than to

> promote a sense of equity and fairness. The elaborate, long-drawn-out
> site screening process which the waste act explicitly and implicitly pre-
> scribes amounts to a cruelly demanding political marathon. (Carter 1987,
> 45)

Carter is correct to assert that, as general rules, Congress ought to want to
limit a search to as few regions as possible and keep the process as simple as
possible. But his view seems to express a lack of appreciation of how difficult those simplifying maneuvers are. In short, Douglas Arnold's view of
high-level nuclear waste site choice cited earlier is the best response to
Carter. Even though the Nevada site emerged in the late 1970s as the leading candidate, it still took legislators a decade to accept this seemingly obvious solution. That it took so long is a result of the central importance of the
nature of the particularistic costs and the opportunities and constraints this
moment in political time offered. That it was resolved at all would seem to
be more of a wonder than the delay.

Practitioners and observers of this process alike frequently assert that
Congress mistakenly allowed "politics" to seep into the process of site selection and that Congress is incapable of handling such issues objectively. For
instance, Gerald Jacob, a critic of the outcome himself, asserts,

> while everyone can appreciate that a complex, highly sophisticated engi-
> neering is required to safely store nuclear materials for thousands of
> years, few have appreciated the political requirements necessary to design
> and implement such a solution. While vast resources have been expend-
> ed on developing complex and sophisticated technologies, the equally
> sophisticated political processes and institutions required to develop a
> credible and legitimate strategy for nuclear waste management have not
> been developed. (Carter 1990, 164)

While Congress's choice of Yucca Mountain may have taken some time and
been short of elegance, it does serve to remind us that legislators need not
wait with bated breath for social scientists to develop new institutional solutions to these types of policy problems. They appear to be quite capable of
developing and implementing them on their own.

FOUR

NAFTA

The pursuit of free trade presents a policy problem very similar to those discussed in the previous chapters. While virtually all economists agree that lowering trade barriers promotes economic growth and reduces prices for consumers, legislators find it difficult to avoid the allure of particularistic protectionism in the absence of procedural restraint. Despite this collective-action problem, however, tariffs have steadily declined over the past sixty years and other non-tariff barriers have been reduced at times as well.

This changed pattern in trade policy[1] is largely the result of the changed procedural context in which trade policy is made and, as in the other cases with which this study has been concerned, we are interested in examining precisely what kinds of procedures are used and why. This chapter will examine the adoption of the North American Free Trade Agreement (NAFTA) and the so-called fast-track procedure employed by Congress to gain additional leverage on the question of procedural choice. NAFTA reduced tariffs and other non-tariff barriers in trade between the United States, Canada, and Mexico, effectively creating a freer North American trading zone. Unlike base closure and nuclear waste, NAFTA presents a policy problem in which Congress is seeking to impose relatively geographically dispersed particularistic costs in a relatively broad policy area. In those two cases, we saw that legislators chose different procedures that allowed them to overcome the collective-action problem they faced. In base closure, legislators delegated a significant amount of authority to an ad hoc institution that would have power to make choices and implement those choices. In the matter of nuclear waste, Congress appeared to delegate some authority, but a closer examination revealed that members of Congress actually delegated very little. That lesson is important in examining NAFTA. The conventional understanding of the enactment of this international agreement is that legislators were able to reduce trade barriers because they delegated authority to the president—an institution that is understood to have more liberal trade preferences because of its national constituency. But, as we will see, the extent to which legislators delegated in the case of NAFTA has been overstated and what delegation there was, was the result of the fact that NAFTA required negotiation with foreign powers. In making this case, it is first necessary to briefly review the history of trade policy in the United States.

A Brief History of U.S. Trade Policy

1789–1930

Among the first powers granted to Congress in Article I, Section 8 of the Constitution are the powers to "lay and collect taxes, duties, imposts and excises" and "to regulate commerce with foreign nations." Because the generation of revenue was wholly dependent in the early days of the republic on these types of taxes, it is not surprising that the first law enacted by Congress was a tariff bill (O'Halloran 1994, 2).[2] From that point on, along with slavery, the tariff became the most important and controversial political issue for more than a century. And for most of that time, it is important to note, tariff policy was considered a domestic matter. Tariffs were enacted to promote industrial development and to raise revenue.

Throughout the nineteenth century, battles over the tariff were fought mainly along sectional lines. The rural and less industrial South was more dependent on imported goods than the North and it was northern industries that primarily benefited from protectionism. Not surprisingly, at the turn of the twentieth century, this meant that the Democratic Party had somewhat more liberal trade preferences while the Republican Party was more protectionist. But even when Democrats were able to gain control of the House, the Senate, and the presidency, trade liberalization was hard to achieve. In 1894, with Democrats in control of Congress and Grover Cleveland in the White House, the Wilson-Gorman Act reduced tariffs modestly, but made only a small dent in the high tariffs instituted by the McKinley Act of 1890. A couple of months later, the Democrats lost control of the House and, in 1896, they lost the Senate and the presidency (Gilligan 1997, 64). In the period between 1890 and 1930, Congress enacted seven major trade bills, only one of which enacted substantial tariff reduction. Indeed, that bill, the Underwood Act of 1913, was enacted with Democrats and Progressives in control of the Congress and the White House, a weakened Speaker in the House (Gilligan 1997, 66), and, not surprisingly, the use of what was "essentially a closed rule" (Gilligan 1997, 1) on the House floor. The period ended with the poster child for particularistic protectionism run amok—the Smoot-Hawley tariff of 1930, which increased duties on over 25,000 specified commodities (O'Halloran 1994, 2–3n2).

1930–1974

The New Deal changed both the form and the substance of American public policy in virtually every policy area, and trade policy was no exception. The signal event of change was the enactment of the Reciprocal Trade Agreements Act of 1934 (RTAA). While the Democrats took control of the Congress and the White House because of the profound economic consequences of the Depression, perhaps no piece of legislation better represented the failed Republican response to the economic calamity than Smoot-Hawley. Among the incumbents who were not returned to Congress were the authors of Smoot-Hawley, Senator Reed Smoot (R-UT) and Representative Willis Hawley (R-OR).[3] When legislators pay that ultimate price, other legislators take note, and the RTAA was the result. The RTAA gave the president power to negotiate and commit the nation to reciprocal trade agreements by executive proclamation. However, the president's power was limited in that the delegation of authority was not permanent (only three years), he could reduce tariffs only by up to 50 percent from 1934 levels, and he could not transfer items between the dutiable and free lists (O'Halloran 1994, 85–86). Nonetheless, despite these limitations, the RTAA stands as a striking example of congressional delegation. Contrary to most observers who view the RTAA as a sharp departure from trade policy procedures of the past, Sharyn O'Halloran argues that there was "a long tradition in U.S. trade policy of delegating authority to the executive branch to negotiate reciprocal concessions." Nevertheless, O'Halloran concedes that while it was "not wholly unconnected to previous trade policy," the RTAA was "a great leap forward" (O'Halloran 1994, 108).

The results of the RTAA program are well known. Between 1934 and 1945, the United States entered into agreements with twenty-eight countries; RTAA was renewed in 1937, 1940, and 1943, and Congress acted in 1945 to give the president authority to reduce rates by an additional 50 percent, permitting a total reduction of 75 percent from 1934 rates. Congress also renewed RTAA authority in 1947, 1948, 1949, 1951, 1953, 1954, 1955, and 1958 (O'Halloran 1994, 87–92). The frequency of these renewals suggests two points. First, legislators found their new role as supervisor of an executive setting rates more appealing than setting the tariff rates themselves. Second, despite the fact that RTAA was consistently renewed, the short terms suggest the short leash on which members of Congress hoped to keep the president. O'Halloran (1994, 108) argues that renewals of the president's negotiating authority

> were anything but automatic. In many instances, as in the one-year extensions of authority in 1947, 1953, and 1954, Congress strongly contested the president's use of his discretionary authority. When imports threatened sensitive domestic industries, Congress introduced new forms of import relief (the escape clause and the peril point provision) to protect disaffected constituents. At each turn, the authorizing legislation showed the effects of partisan conflict and a willingness on the part of legislators to design complex procedures that protected specific industries.

The resulting trend in tariffs was also easy to spot. While in the period between the Civil War and the New Deal, the ratio of total tariff receipts to total dutiable imports had been around .4 to .5, the ratio declined steadily after the enactment of RTAA and hovered throughout the 1950s and 1960s at about .1 (Gilligan 1997, 1–2).

In 1962, President Kennedy asked for and received new negotiating authority. The Congress gave the president broad powers to pursue tariff reductions and removed some of the impediments to trade negotiations by providing avenues of compensation for injured industries rather than exempting them from coverage. This new negotiating authority set the stage for the first multilateral trade negotiations under the General Agreement on Tariffs and Trade (GATT)—a negotiating round that reduced average duties by about 35 percent. But conflict broke out between the Johnson administration and the Congress over whether non-tariff trade barriers should be part of the trade talks (O'Halloran 1994, 95–96). The conflict remained unresolved and the president's negotiating authority became a victim of the impasse. When the authority conferred in 1962 lapsed, no new authority was granted over the next several years.

1974–1988

The 1974 Trade Reform Act marked a dramatic procedural shift in American trade policy. By the end of the Kennedy–Johnson round of tariff reductions, it had become increasingly clear that tariffs no longer presented the major threat to free trade. Instead, non-tariff barriers were the concern and this posed a new challenge. Non-tariff barriers are defined by what they are not rather than what they are, and that observation suggests a problem with breaking them down. Because the category contains a wide variety of trade practices, delegating authority to the president to unilaterally reduce these barriers would be far too wide a delegation of power. Moreover, as we have discussed in previous chapters, the early 1970s were not a period in American political history in which legislators were particularly inclined to delegate additional power to the president. As a result, since 1974, though non-tariff barriers have been the subject of international trade negotiations, presidents have been unable to enter into international trade agreements without congressional approval. The Trade Reform Act gave birth to the so-called fast-track procedure in which Congress would have to approve any international trade agreement before it became binding, but, in return, Congress would have to consider the agreement under expedited legislative procedures that did not allow for any amendments. Congress also gave itself a greater role in trade negotiations in a variety of ways that we will discuss in greater detail later and created the Office of the Special Representative for Trade Negotiations to be headed by the U.S. Trade Representative (USTR). In addition to conducting negotiations with trade partners, the USTR would investigate alleged unfair trade practices such as foreign import restrictions, export subsidies, and dumping; section 301 of the Act authorized the president to unilaterally retaliate against these practices.

The 1974 Act paved the way for the Tokyo round of GATT negotiations. When Congress acted to approve the agreement in 1979, they also enacted a slightly modified extension of the new trade procedures for eight years. In 1984, Congress again amended these procedures, allowing the Ways and Means and Finance Committees to revoke fast-track authority within sixty days after the president notified Congress of his intention to enter into trade negotiations. Moreover, Congress took steps to bolster its own power in the wake of the *Chadha* decision, which had taken away Congress's power to unilaterally force the president to retaliate against unfair trade practices. Congress responded by shifting the authority to initiate unfair trade practices cases to the USTR.

In 1988, when Congress extended fast-track authority for three more years with the option of an additional two years if neither house passed a disapproval resolution, Congress took both the 1984 provisions strengthening Congress's role a step further by adding a so-called reverse fast-track procedure in which Congress could revoke fast-track authority by passing a disapproval resolution in both houses within any sixty-day period and by transferring to the USTR (from the president) the authority to unilaterally retaliate against unfair trade practices. The 1988 law put in place the final piece of the procedural context in which NAFTA would be negotiated and eventually approved.

While this historical tour has been brief, it has served to highlight an important point that will be emphasized throughout the rest of this chapter. The standard interpretation that American trade policy has become increasingly liberalized as a result of congressional abdication of authority during the sixty years prior to the enactment of NAFTA is simplistic at best and inaccurate at worst. The procedures by which international trade agreements are negotiated, approved, and implemented are far more complicated and provide far more procedural power to Congress than is commonly understood. We will examine the complexity of these procedures in more detail later, but first, it is useful to take a step back and understand the collective-action problem Congress is seeking to resolve with these complex procedures in the first place.

The Problem of Protectionism and Trade Policy

The problem posed by trade policy is one that is not unfamiliar to us. Free trade reduces prices for consumers by eliminating tariffs and other non-tariff costs to producers that are usually passed on to consumers. Free trade also encourages greater competition and innovation by leveling the playing field for producers. Of course, members of Congress would all like to be associated with the benefits of free trade, but they are also eager to protect the particular industries based in their districts from foreign competition. Because no single legislator can protect the industries in their district on their own, the result is a collective logroll in which universalistic protectionism triumphs over free trade. The nation would be collectively better off with reciprocal trade agreements reducing trade barriers, but members of Congress have individual incentives that are collectively destructive.

Political economists have long been aware that collective-action problems are a key feature of normal trade politics. While Mancur Olson published his seminal study on the sources of collective-action problems in 1965, Michael Gilligan points out that Olson himself outlined the implications of his theory for trade politics in his 1982 work, *The Rise and Decline of Nations.* Gilligan (1997, 4) summarizes the logic:

> Since import competing industries form a much smaller group than consumers do they have much less stringent collective-action problems and can more readily take political action. Furthermore, producer groups can sometimes provide selective incentives such as closed shops or profes-

sional licensing requirements that consumer groups cannot. As such there is a bias in the political system in favor of protectionism.

Following this argument to its logical endpoint, various scholars point out that presidents will therefore have more liberal trade preferences than Congress. Robert Baldwin (1998, 81–82) argues that the presidential bias in favor of free trade is the result of the foreign policy responsibilities associated with the office. Presidents seek to advance their national security agenda (this was true particularly during the cold war) by promoting closer economic ties with foreign powers. While this argument has some merit, it is more likely that presidents have more liberal trade preferences than members of Congress for the same reason presidents are more likely to support base closures, tax reform, and the choice of a site—any site—for high-level nuclear waste disposal. A president is one person representing a national constituency and therefore does not suffer from the collective-action problems that plague Congress. The natural answer, then, would appear to be delegation. With members of Congress "torn between their free-trade proclivities and the protectionist demands of their constituents" (Wiarda 1994, 131), the president is "in a better position to weigh the overall costs and benefits of protectionism" (O'Halloran 1994, 32). This theory squares with our anecdotes and observations of trade politics in action. In pushing for the passage of the enabling legislation for NAFTA, President Clinton even promised to defend congressional Republican incumbents against Democratic challengers who attack them for their votes supporting the agreement. Recognizing the collective-action problem at work, Clinton declared, "I do not believe that any member of Congress should be defeated for doing what is plainly in the national interest."[4]

Why Study NAFTA?

The collective-action problem described above applies to any trade agreement. Therefore, to discuss NAFTA seems appropriate because of its temporal proximity to the other cases examined in this study. However, NAFTA is also a particularly attractive case for study because there are several reasons why it presented a particularly difficult problem for free trade-minded legislators.

First, taking down trade barriers with Mexico is fundamentally different from removing such barriers with more economically advanced trading partners. As *Congressional Quarterly* (1997, 153) has pointed out, "it was the first time the United States had agreed to take down all economic walls guarding it from a country whose economy was as poor and as different from its own as Mexico's." Timothy McKeown (1994, 67) makes the argument more directly in his assessment of how interest groups impact American trade policy.

> The least painful and most valuable agreement is one between two countries whose production is complementary, and whose consumption patterns create a large demand for the products of the other country. Increased competitive pressure on import-competing industries, such as that faced by American lumber from Canadian imports or by American low-wage manufacturing . . . from Mexican imports, creates economic adjustment costs and political opposition to agreements.

McKeown also points out a second reason why NAFTA represented a particularly tough case. He argues, "evidence is accumulating that for firms, nations, or the international system as a whole, growth does create the political conditions for trade openness, while the lack of growth does the opposite" (1994, 71). The American economy was growing when legislators decided to delegate authority to the president to negotiate NAFTA, but it went into a recession while the pact was being negotiated and this altered the politics of the negotiation. O'Halloran (1994, 159) points out that because of the recession, a number of industries were more sensitive to import competition:

> The most vocal opposition to the proposed free-trade agreement came from fruit and vegetable producers, textile and apparel manufacturers, auto suppliers, and the steel industry, all of whose products competed directly with Mexican imports. This opposition was even more difficult to ignore in hard economic times.

And this leads to a third reason NAFTA represented a particularly difficult problem for legislators. Whereas the Republicans had been the majority party in the Senate in 1986 when Congress gave a Republican president fast-track authority to negotiate a trade agreement with Canada, the Democrats held majorities in both the House and the Senate throughout the negotiation and approval of NAFTA. The importance of unions in the Democratic coalition and the importance of the steel, textile, and auto industries in parts of the nation that Democratic members of Congress tend to represent meant that NAFTA would face a particularly difficult path.

Fourth, and related to the prior point, legislators are less likely to give authority to a president of a different party. O'Halloran (1994, 35) argues,

> If a principal could find a perfectly representative agent, she could obtain her ideal outcome by delegating completely to the agent. One corollary to this observation is that the greater the difference in preferences between the principal and the agent, the less authority will be delegated. If we take partisanship as a proxy for preferences, then the implications for trade policy are clear. Congress will delegate more power to a president of the same party than to a president of the opposing party.

McKeown (1994, 72) echoes this view, arguing, "when the presidency is controlled by an opposing party, delegation is less likely, since the preferences of the president on trade are more likely to be different than those of the party which controls Congress." One result of this principle in action is the creation of the reverse fast-track procedure. Democratic congressional leaders were less than pleased with the level of consultation they had been accorded during the negotiation of the U.S.–Canadian Free Trade Agreement (O'Halloran 1994, 159–60). They responded by adding the reverse fast-track provision for the negotiation of NAFTA that allowed the Congress to revoke fast-track authority if both houses of Congress enacted a resolution within any sixty-day period.

A final reason NAFTA was a more difficult agreement to enact than the standard collective-action problem associated with free trade is that any agreement would require that regulatory structures be erected in a deregulatory era. Because tariffs had been reduced to such low levels under the RTAA program, those who promote free trade have been far more focused on reducing non-tariff trade barriers in the past twenty-five years. The promotion of free trade in the 1980s and 1990s thus requires regulatory structures that will monitor, investigate, and fight unfair trade practices undertaken by foreign competitors. The enhanced powers and roles of the USTR discussed above are the result of this new emphasis. The importance of this regulatory paradox for our purposes, however, is that it serves as yet another reason why NAFTA was even more difficult to enact than the traditional collective-action theories would suggest. Pietro Nivola (1993, 15) argues,

> Not only did much regulation of foreign trade practices take root amid a policy dissensus; it expanded during a period of growing awareness and sophistication about the limitations of other economic regulatory ventures. While the U.S. government was policing more international

commerce, it curtailed its role in important sectors of the domestic economy, areas such as transportation, energy, and telecommunications.

Given all these difficulties, it is not surprising that NAFTA became "the most contentious piece of trade legislation of the twentieth century" (Gilligan 1997, 82). More than a difficult collective-action problem, NAFTA was a trade agreement that required legislators to delegate authority during a recession to a president from the opposing party to negotiate a trade pact with a neighbor whose economy was far less industrialized; moreover, it was an agreement that would regulate commerce during an anti-regulatory era. Before examining how reelection-minded legislators accomplished this herculean task, it is useful first to examine the provisions of NAFTA as enacted so that we can better understand where the process was headed.

The Provisions of NAFTA

The NAFTA-implementing legislation cleared the House on November 17, 1993, cleared the Senate on November 20, 1993, and was signed into law by President Clinton on December 8 of that year.[5] The major provisions of NAFTA significantly liberalized trade between the United States, Canada, and Mexico. The legislation gave the president authority to make tariff reductions specified in the agreement, lifted import quota restrictions on a variety of Mexican agricultural products, and liberalized some U.S. agricultural standards. In addition, the agreement liberalized U.S. government procurement procedures making some government contracts available to Mexican bidders, qualified automobiles manufactured in Canada or Mexico as domestically produced if 75 percent of the cost of the car was value added in North America, and established trade dispute-settlement procedures (*Congressional Quarterly* 1997, 159–61).

While these major provisions of NAFTA effectively created a much freer zone of trade between the United States, Mexico, and Canada, the details of the legislation also contained a variety of provisions that denied pure free traders a complete victory. The legislation established mechanisms to protect U.S. industries from floods of imports in much the same way the U.S.–Canada Free Trade Agreement had a few years earlier. The president was empowered to suspend tariff reductions on certain products if the International Trade Commission determined the imports to be a serious threat to a domestic industry. The legislation also included a special expedited mechanism to protect the American orange juice industry. Moreover, while certain American agricultural standards were relaxed, the standards for certain products such as peanut butter still had to meet U.S. standards. Finally, the legislation also provided transitional worker assistance to workers hurt by NAFTA, codified side agreements negotiated by the Clinton administration on labor and the environment, authorized the funding of a Center for the Study of Western Hemispheric Trade, and authorized American participation in the North American Development Bank, which would fund border cleanup and economic development projects.

In the remainder of this chapter, we will outline a number of other ways in which NAFTA is not simply a case of legislators voting for free trade over particularistic protectionism. But the general theme of the major provisions of NAFTA should not be lost. NAFTA did create a significantly liberalized trading zone between the United States, Canada, and Mexico. Legislators who, according to the textbook understanding of legislative behavior, were worried that constituents would fail to notice the benefits of NAFTA and to connect those benefits with their vote, indeed did vote to liberalize trade. How? As we have seen in the other cases with which this study is concerned, specialized legislative procedures allowed Congress to overcome this collective-action problem.

Procedures as Key

In her examination of how trade policy is made, Sharyn O'Halloran suggests that many students of trade policy emphasize the ways in which interest groups seek favorable treatment while others focus on the role played by executive agencies. On this scholarhip, O'Halloran (1994, ix) points out,

> Each of these approaches certainly captures an important element of how policy is made, but before they can be effectively evaluated, we must first ask: What procedures define the decision-making process, and what effect do they have on public policy? The choice of institutions is a political one and is crucial to determining outcomes.

While few political scientists would dispute O'Halloran's argument, there remains a great deal of misunderstanding about the nature of the procedures used in the case of NAFTA and the degree to which those procedures delegate authority to the executive. As we have discussed, most scholars view trade policy as a case where Congress recognizes its own institutional shortcomings in dealing with a difficult collective-action problem and delegates authority to presidents who are more likely to make policy consistent with the general interest. As we will see, this view is far too simplistic; but before tackling that theoretical question, it is useful first to review some of the details of the fast-track procedure adopted for NAFTA and the way in which this procedure has been understood by most scholars.

The Omnibus Trade and Competitiveness Act of 1988[6] authorized the president to negotiate bilateral and multilateral trade agreements that would be submitted for congressional approval under expedited procedures that would guarantee an up-or-down vote without amendments. The law also allowed the president to request a two-year extension of fast-track authority that would be automatically granted unless either the House or the Senate adopted a resolution of disapproval.

Most observers have viewed this fast-track procedure as a congressional abdication of authority. The best example of this view is the work of I. M. Destler, who argues,

> for the great majority of members to whom trade is but an occasional concern, it is sufficient to advocate the cause of constituent groups important in one's district—and the national extensions of these groups, and to strike general trade-policy postures which appeal to one's support coalitions. For most members in most instances, it is simply not cost-effective to strive for direct, significant personal influence over trade-policy outcomes. Nor is such influence necessary to the member. Mayhew [1974] points to three activities typical of reelection-seeking Representatives: advertising, position-taking, and credit-claiming. None of these requires actual impact on policy. (Destler 1998, 98)

It is particularly appropriate that Destler links his view of American trade policymaking to Mayhew since this study is linked to the critique of the Mayhewian (1974) model of legislative behavior offered by Douglas Arnold. In any case, Destler's view of how trade policy is made under fast track is clear. Presidents and executive agencies dominate the process because legislators abdicate their authority, seeking only symbolic victories. Before Congress gave away its power in this policy area, Destler argues, industries seeking protection had to come to Congress for assistance.

> Now, they must seek that action elsewhere. Legislation still matters to them, of course: it can establish rules, set priorities, make import relief (or export-market-opening action) easier or harder to obtain. And constituencies still matter to Congress: representing them is something mem-

bers and their staffs take very seriously. But Congress has tied members' hands regarding their ability to legislate constituency-specific trade measures. So if it is effective, product-specific trade policy action these constituents want, they are unlikely to get it on Capitol Hill. Non-binding resolutions backing semiconductor makers in their fight for Japanese markets? Certainly. Textile quota bills for the President to veto? Of course. Advice on who to talk to at USTR or Commerce? Sure. But something real? Not likely. (Destler 1998, 95)

While Destler's view of congressional authority in trade policy is commonplace, it fails to recognize the variety of subtle and not so subtle ways that fast-track procedures allow members of Congress to influence the process. A more detailed look at the particular procedure utilized to enact NAFTA reinforces this view.

One aspect of this procedure that has received scant attention is the fact that NAFTA was negotiated and adopted as a congressional-executive agreement rather than as a treaty. It is a little-mentioned fact that NAFTA was passed by the Senate by a vote of 61–38, several votes short of the two-thirds majority necessary to approve a treaty. This prompts Bruce Ackerman and David Golove to ask,

Whatever happened to the Treaty Clause? No less puzzling is why this obvious question was never raised during the long hard battle over NAFTA. The opponents were grimly determined to gain victory at all costs. They could well have mustered the thirty-four Senators needed to defeat NAFTA if it had been treated as a treaty rather than a congressional-executive agreement. And yet the obvious questions were left unasked. (Ackerman and Golove 1995, 1–2)

Ackerman and Golove review the history of the evolution of the process by which Congress and the president negotiate and approve international agreements. Their argument is important for our purposes because they point out that there was nothing inevitable about the evolution of this procedure. The Constitution, they argue, puts in place three distinct legislative systems: law making, treaty approval, and the process for constitutional amendments. The existence of these three distinct systems, however, begs the question of interchangeability. They pose the following questions:

To what degree could statute-making substitute for treaty-writing, and vice versa? The Supremacy Clause provides part of an answer by stipulating that a treaty could serve as the "law of the land" and take immediate effect as a federal law. But the text is not equally clear about the opposite relationship. Could a majority of both Houses, in the exercise of its statute-making powers, approve international agreements? The Treaty Clause does not say Yes or No, and so constitutionalists are left to construe the sounds of silence. (Ackerman and Golove 1995, 8)

The point is relevant to our discussion because it is only relatively recently that the answer has become a clear yes. During and after World War II, informal precedents were set that allowed for the interchangeability of the statute-making and treaty processes for international agreements despite the failure of parallel efforts to adopt a constitutional amendment explicitly authorizing this interchangeability. The Trade Act of 1974 further codified the process grafting fast-track procedures onto the congressional-executive agreement process.

Seen in this light, fast-track procedures are an enhancement of congressional capacity and authority rather than an abdication of power as Destler claims. If NAFTA had been considered as a treaty, for instance, it is highly plausible that a minority of senators would have been able to kill the agreement. And because the treaty procedure offers legislators no formal opportunity to influence the treaty in its formative stages, it is no surprise that treaty approval debates are so contentious. In contrast, as we will see, fast-track procedures encourage and facilitate congressional input in the negotiating stages while simultaneously empowering majorities in both houses at the expense of a minority in the Senate. In Ackerman and Golove's (1995, 105) terms, "the classic constitutional procedure not only generates unnecessary disaffection abroad but encourages obfuscation at home. The Trade Act strikes at these practices, but succeeds only because it encourages interbranch consultation at the policy formulation stage."

The notion that members of Congress simply throw up their arms and delegate authority to the executive to dominate trade policy isn't even logically consistent. Michael Gilligan (1997, 5) asks tough questions of those who believe Congress delegates authority to get around the collective-action problem associated with trade policy that are particularly relevant to this study. First,

if Congress was unable to resist constituency pressures in order to liberalize trade policy itself, why was it able to resist them to make an institutional change that led to liberalization? It is also hard to see how delegation could in any way insulate Congress from constituency pressures. Congress was still faced with periodic renewals of the president's delegated authority.

Second, and more importantly for the purposes of this study, Gilligan (1997, 5) asks, "if a universalistic logroll was the source of the problem why did Congress choose delegation rather than one of several other institutional innovations that also would have cured it?" The answer to the question, of course, is that Congress did not delegate in the case of NAFTA to overcome a collective-action problem. Rather, Congress delegated authority to the president because the nature of the policy problem required that *someone* negotiate with a foreign power.

Indeed, when we look closely at the fast-track procedure utilized for NAFTA, we see a variety of ways in which legislators restricted the authority that was delegated and made sure that their preferences would be taken into account in any agreement. A number of the more restrictive provisions adopted for the NAFTA negotiations were the result of congressional displeasure with the president's handling of previously delegated authority. For instance, in the Omnibus Trade and Competitiveness Act of 1988, the law that put the fast-track procedures for NAFTA in place, Congress added so-called super 301 amendments that transferred authority to conduct investigations into unfair trade practices from the president to the USTR, required the USTR to provide Congress with reports on countries engaged in unfair trade practices, and required mandatory trade retaliation if a country was found to be engaging in unfair trade practices.

But what are the procedures by which Congress maintains control over trade policy while delegating authority to the president to negotiate trade deals? The obvious aspect of fast track that gives Congress authority is the fact that an international agreement requires positive congressional action in order to take effect. Because this forces legislators to make a binary choice between an agreement and no agreement, legislators find it easier to justify a vote for free trade over protectionism. Pietro Nivola argues:

> The assumption that the American trade policy process suffers whenever Congress is presented with a polarizing choice is questionable. An administration defending a regime of liberal trade may wind up better off debating its dissidents than trying too hard to co-opt them. The reason is quite simple: most lawmakers are not anxious to restore outmoded protectionism. They remain conscious that a reprise of the Smoot-Hawley syndrome would constitute, in the words of Senator John C. Danforth, "an act of gross stupidity." (Nivola 1993, 149)

But the fast-track process offers legislators far more control than a mere up-or-down vote on an agreement negotiated by the president. Though it is not well-known or frequently pointed out by scholars who view fast track as a tool of presidential dominance, Congress retained several other formal tools at its disposal to derail NAFTA. First, though Congress delegated fast-track negotiating authority to the president in 1988, the president is required to notify Congress before entering into negotiations with any nation. Within the next sixty days, if *either* the House Ways and Means *or* the Senate Finance Committee passes a resolution disapproving the negotiations, fast-track authority is revoked. The president is, of course, free to negotiate with whomever he wants, whenever he wants. But those negotiations are unlikely to be fruitful if Congress has not agreed to vote on an agreement without amendments. Effectively, then, Congress instituted a one-committee legislative veto over trade negotiations. Assuming Congress does not exercise this option, it still retains the option of stopping the negotiations at any point through use of the so-called reverse fast-track procedure. If both the full House and the full Senate pass a disapproval resolution within any sixty-day period, fast-track authority is revoked. These reverse fast-track procedures thus constitute a second legislative veto—a two-house legislative veto—over fast-track negotiations. Finally, as discussed earlier, even though Congress provided for an automatic two-year extension of fast-track authority in the authorizing legislation, that two-year extension could be revoked if either house of Congress voted a simple resolution disapproving of the extension within a ninety-day period once the president requested the extension. Effectively, this would provide a third legislative veto—this time a one-house veto—that members of Congress could use to kill the negotiations altogether.

These formal procedures that Congress could use to pressure the administration were supplemented with procedural requirements that would provide members of Congress with an insider's view of the negotiations as they proceeded. The president was required, for instance, to provide the International Trade Commission with a list of articles to be discussed in negotiations before any agreement was negotiated. The Omnibus Trade and Competitiveness Act also created a host of private sector advisory committees that would advise negotiators and attend negotiating sessions to keep an eye on issues that might affect their particular industries. In addition, Congress instituted significant reporting requirements on both the USTR and these private sector advisory committees. Finally, members of Congress ensured their own physical presence at negotiating sessions by allowing the Speaker of the House and the president of the Senate to appoint congressional delegates to the negotiations.

The purpose of all these requirements is clear. As O'Halloran describes it, these procedures created

> an elaborate "fire-alarm" oversight mechanism that incorporates the private sector, government agencies, and even congressional committees in developing international trade agreements. These consultations serve two purposes. First, groups sensitive to or threatened by the proposed agreement are given an opportunity to express their concerns and seek compensation. Second, negotiators learn from these consultations which are the industries that, if ignored, may lobby members of Congress to veto any eventual agreement. (O'Halloran 1994, 144–45)

A number of less formal arrangements also allow members of Congress to impact trade policy. First, even though Congress is required under fast-track procedures to vote up or down without amendments within ninety days on the agreement as negotiated by the president, the House Ways and Means and Senate Finance Committees do hold mock mark-up sessions on the implementing legislation, which provides an opportunity for legislators not only to learn more about what is in the agreement but to also strike side deals with the administration in return for their support. It was at this point in the process, for instance, that the Clinton administration agreed to add worker retraining money to the NAFTA implementing bill (*Congressional Quarterly* 1997, 157).

All these procedural requirements add up to real congressional influence over trade negotiations without allowing legislators' protectionist proclivities to run rampant. President Bush expressed his intention to negotiate a trade agreement with Canada and Mexico in September 1990, which meant he would need the automatic two-year extension of fast-track authority as the original grant of authority would expire in May 1991 if either house of Congress voted a simple resolution to deny the extension. Each house had a tough debate on a resolution in May 1991 in which the vote to extend fast-track authority was widely viewed as a referendum on NAFTA. And while the House rejected the disapproval resolution by a vote of 192–231 and the Senate by a vote of 36–59 (*Congressional Quarterly* 1993, 189), the episode demonstrated the importance of the procedural hurdle in ensuring congressional influence. O'Halloran (1994, 161–62) points out that the Congress "took the opportunity of the renewal of fast track to ensure that many of the most controversial issues—the environment, labor concerns, and workers' rights—were written directly into the authorizing legislation." Specifically, the Congress insisted on a variety of safeguard and transition provisions that would reduce barriers slowly and provide for the restoration of barriers with escape clauses if domestic industries faced significant damage. The president was also forced to agree to a domestic-content rule for cars of more than 50 percent. Finally, the president also vowed "not to negotiate lower standards than were currently in the law in the areas of pesticides, energy conservation, toxic waste, and health and safety" (O'Halloran 1994, 163).

While O'Halloran correctly criticizes the dominant presidency-centered understanding of how trade policy is made, it is important to note that many other observers also seem to recognize the greater role played by Congress as a result of fast-track procedures. Because many of these authors tend to view presidential dominance as a normative good, their tone on this effect of fast-track procedures is decidedly different. But it is unmistakably the same view of congressional influence. Robert Baldwin, for instance, complains that

> one consequence of the new implementing procedures is that members of Congress and various special interests have become involved in the negotiations at a micro-management level. Under the threat of the rejection of the agreement by Congress, administration officials have sometimes been pressured into negotiating detailed provisions that favor a particular interest group at the welfare cost of the general public. (Baldwin 1998, 79)

Similarly, Ackerman and Golove argue that under fast-track procedures,

> no longer can legislators escape their moment of truth, yet both Senators and Representatives are given many opportunities to voice their concerns and threaten the executive with the prospect of ultimate defeat should their advice be ignored. (Ackerman and Golove 1995, 106)

Michael Gilligan takes this argument a step further by suggesting that the only reason legislators delegate authority in the first place is because they are seeking to reduce *foreign* trade barriers and this requires the assistance of an executive.[7] Finally, O'Halloran (1994, 5) views fast-track procedures as an explicit attempt "to ensure that the actions taken by the president are in line with legislators' preferences." In defending this view, O'Halloran points out that

> I do not go as far as congressional dominance theorists in insisting that Congress always gets its way; after all, one central reason for delegating authority is to make policy different from what Congress would have

passed on its own. But I do recognize that Congress has the constitutional authority to regulate commerce, and therefore any executive authority in this area is delegated authority and should be analyzed as such. (O'Halloran 1994, 36)

Applying the Theory: Procedural Choice and NAFTA

We have seen in the preceding section that the subtle details of fast-track procedures and the extent to which those procedures allow for congressional influence in trade negotiations have been underappreciated. Both these points speak directly to the central question with which this study is concerned. Why do legislators choose the particular procedures they do in attempting to overcome collective-action problems? Answering this question in the case of NAFTA requires returning to the propositions we have examined in each of the other cases.

Proposition I. Geographic Concentration of Costs

Few observers of trade policy doubt that geography matters. Destler (1998, 93) points out that the trade literature "has established, beyond a reasonable doubt, the responsiveness of individual members to constituent interests concentrated within their districts." This behavior is nothing new, of course. In discussing the relative advantage heavy industry had over agricultural producers in securing reciprocal trade provisions late in the nineteenth century, Gilligan (1997, 11) argues that "factors inherent in industrial production put industry in a much better position to overcome collective-action problems and lobby the government than agriculture enjoyed." What were those factors? He responds,

> Industry was geographically concentrated in a few states in the Northeast and the eastern Great Lakes region of the country. Agriculture was spread over hundreds of thousands of square miles throughout the country often in areas of great isolation where communication was very difficult. (Gilligan 1997, 11)

In a study of the politics of protectionism in the 1970s and 1980s, Wendy Hansen (1990, 36) tested the hypothesis that "more political power is generated when an industry is geographically concentrated in a relatively small number of states or congressional districts." When she examined the relative level of protection afforded industries whose operations were concentrated in a small number of states, she found that those whose operations were concentrated received more protection.

While all these authors agree, then, that legislators afford greater protection to interests that are geographically concentrated, scholars who view fast-track procedures as a scheme of presidential dominance argue that Congress overcomes its collective-action problem by delegating authority to the president to lower trade barriers across industrial boundaries. Destler, for instance, argues,

> For sixty-plus years, Congress has simultaneously been yielding power on trade and approving major liberalizing initiatives. It has done so while regularly sounding protectionist-enabling liberal traders to warn regularly of the wolf at their door. But somehow the wolf never gets in. Of if he does, he spares most of the sheep. (Destler 1998, 96)

But this view is far too simplistic. As discussed above, in adopting fast-track procedures, members of Congress are not simply accepting that they cannot play a reasonable part in trade policy and therefore ceding control over the policy area to the president. On the contrary, just as we will see later in the case of tax reform, members of Congress designed procedures that would allow them to lower trade barriers while protecting the most sensitive of trade benefits—those that are geographically concentrated. They instituted numerous fire-alarm oversight mechanisms to ensure that private groups could alert Congress during the negotiations to potential negative policy impacts before any agreement was signed. Legislators also designed fast-track procedures in such a way that they would have a number of formal avenues and opportunities to suspend the negotiations if the president deviated too far from congressional preferences. In sum, while Destler indicates that Congress has been involved in a symbolic game, O'Halloran suggests a more sophisticated understanding of congressional behavior:

> Congress's solution has been to temper its delegation, diluting it with procedures through which industries can seek compensation from the adverse effects of increased competition. Thus, instead of Congress legislating itself out of the business of making product-specific trade laws, it has gone into the business of procedural protectionism. (O'Halloran 1994, 180)

This latter point is undoubtedly a reference to arguments such as that made by Pietro Nivola (1993) in *Regulating Unfair Trade*. Nivola argues that legislators seeking to protect individual industries have turned away from erecting trade barriers and toward constructing regulatory structures to fight foreign trade practices deemed unfair. The same argument can be made in the case of fast-track procedures. Legislators, as we will see, have found a way to delegate authority to the president to negotiate lower trade barriers while maintaining enough influence over the president to guarantee that the most geographically concentrated industries will continue to receive preferential treatment.

In the particular case of NAFTA, one clear indicator of the importance of the geographic concentration of trade benefits was the relative difficulty in adopting the enabling legislation for the agreement on the House and Senate floors. Timothy McKeown argues,

> If, as some argue, representatives of small districts have a greater tendency to support policies that create costly spill-overs for other districts (such as federal construction projects), then the Senate ought to be on average less protectionist than the House. (McKeown 1994, 72)

This dynamic played itself out when the enabling legislation for NAFTA came to a vote in the House on November 17, 1993 and in the Senate on November 20, 1993. Senators approved the bill 61–38 while House members approved it by a narrower margin of 234–200. *Congressional Quarterly* explained the difference in voting this way:

> The margin of victory in the Senate was larger in part because senators were less susceptible to the pressures that caused many House members to vote no. Most states were expected to derive some benefit from free trade with Mexico; that was certainly not the case with every House district. For example, two of labor's strongest Democratic allies—Edward M. Kennedy of Massachusetts and Tom Harkin of Iowa—backed the agreement because Mexico offered export opportunities for their states' high-technology or agricultural exports. (*Congressional Quarterly* 1997, 159)

Legislators in both houses also displayed the institution's geographical sensitivity by voting largely along geographical lines. In considering an extension of the president's fast-track negotiating authority in 1991, *Congressional Quarterly* (1993, 189) reported the House was divided "more along regional than party lines." Members from the West and southern border states, the southeastern sunbelt, and the Midwest tended to support the measure while those from areas with large numbers of union workers and non-Mexican immigrants, and heavy manufacturing sectors tended to oppose it. Recognizing the geographic sensitivity of the vote, Democratic House leaders essentially declared members free to vote their consciences. House Speaker Tom Foley (D-WA) supported the pact while the Majority Leader, Richard Gephardt (D-MO), and the Majority Whip, David Bonior (D-MI), both opposed it. Rather than voting their consciences, it would have been more accurate to say members were free to vote their constituencies. While business interests spent millions of dollars attempting to convince wavering members to vote for the pact, President Clinton told business leaders late in October 1993 that their lobbying strategy was not working. He argued,

> Ask your employees who support this to contact their members of Congress. I've had as many Republican as Democratic members of Congress that I am lobbying say to me, "I want to hear from the people that work for the employers, not just from the employers."[8]

In short, geographic constituencies mattered. Because the particular procedures employed required positive congressional approval, the agent to whom power had been delegated was forced to negotiate an agreement that protected at least some of those particular interests.

While fast-track procedures allowed members of Congress a greater degree of influence and input on NAFTA while it was being negotiated than is commonly recognized, they also allowed for a great deal more congressional influence than is commonly recognized *even after* it was negotiated. Indeed, a significant number of members were convinced to support the measure as a result of last-minute concessions that offered geographically concentrated benefits. The Clinton administration was forced to negotiate a side deal before the enabling legislation could be passed "to reinterpret the language of the original pact to restrict trade in sugar and orange juice" (Bradsher 1993, A21). The orange juice provisions bought a number of votes in Florida, while the sugar provisions bought votes in Louisiana and Maryland. Representatives from Tennessee were appeased when the president included their suggestion in the enabling legislation that only whisky produced in Tennessee could be labeled "Bourbon Whisky" or "Tennessee Whisky" (O'Halloran 1994, 170). Representative Tom Lewis (R-FL) would support the pact once the administration agreed to include tomatoes on the list of crops subject to tariffs if imports began flooding the market; two House members from Oklahoma wheat-growing districts agreed to support the pact after the president added teeth to a promise to work toward ending Canadian government subsidies for the transportation and marketing of Canadian wheat (Bradsher 1993, A21). Other members held out for particularistic trade benefits for their districts. Representative Esteban Torres (D-CA) led the way in getting an initial endowment of $4 billion for the North American Development Bank—an institution created by the trade pact that would provide border cleanup and development funds (O'Halloran 1994, 171). And lawmakers in Texas got administration support for a $10 million trade policy research center. Still other lawmakers held out for benefits that had nothing to do with trade at all. *Congressional Quarterly* reported,

> After announcing his support for the NAFTA bill, Floyd H. Flake, D-N.Y., got a call from Clinton telling him that a Small Business Administration pilot program would be located in his Queens district. The White House also agreed to let a dredging project go forward at Jones Beach on Long Island in response to a request by NAFTA backer Peter T. King, R-N.Y. (*Congressional Quarterly* 1997, 158)

In short, the process was a congressional logroll at its best. And, importantly for our purposes, this was clearly the only way something like this could be done. Members with concentrated geographic costs had to be compensated. Representative Tom Lewis (R-FL) complained that the administration had waited until the last minute to strike its deal with him. "I look with disdain on the way this whole thing has been done," he said. "It almost looks like you're selling your soul."[9] Representative Glenn English (D-OK), one of the members who switched his vote as a result of the wheat concession, argued, "It's not a question of buying votes. This is the only way we could have supported the agreement."[10] Thus, though they had different opinions of the process, both legislators would agree that the process worked because members had an opportunity to protect the most sensitive of particularistic benefits—those that are geographically concentrated.

Proposition II. Scope of the Policy Area

International trade agreements in general, and NAFTA in particular, clearly represent what this study has defined as broad policy areas. In pointing out the difficulty of negotiating a pact as significant as NAFTA, Howard Wiarda states that trade negotiators must certainly yearn for the good old days:

> Tariffs used to be the main concern, but this was a subject that was remote from most people's consciousness and without high political

stakes or even visibility. A handful of experts and interest groups got together, hammered out their differences if necessary, and worked out an agreement. But now, the U.S. and Mexican trade negotiators must also deal with "hot" or "new agenda" political topics such as pollution, the environment, drugs, human rights, and democratization. In addition, the negotiators must deal with subjects such as farm and industrial subsidies, patents and trademarks, industrial standards, child labor, minimum wages, unionization and labor rights, government purchasing, and investment issues—all areas that are close to the bone of national economic policymaking. (Wiarda 1994, 119)

Given the breathtaking breadth of this policy area, one is led to wonder, as I. M. Destler does, why legislators would delegate. As we will see, in the similarly broad policy area of tax policy, legislators never even considered delegating authority as a solution to their collective action problem. Though Destler steadfastly, and incorrectly, asserts that Congress yields virtually all control over trade policy to the president, he seems to wonder aloud at one point why Congress would do this in such a broad policy area and concludes, correctly, that the congressional delegation of authority has something to do with the fact that trade agreements are mechanisms of foreign policy. He finds it difficult to,

offer a serious explanation of why Congress behaves rather differently on, say, tax policy—where the same Congressional committees are much more prone to assert their power and distribute particularist benefits. Part of the explanation may be that our domestic trade policymaking system evolved under the international auspices of the GATT, now the WTO. This creates an international constraint on national policy and reinforces the role of the President in the U.S. policy process. (Destler 1998, 100)

While Destler overstates the degree to which Congress has delegated authority, Gilligan agrees that it is this foreign policy dimension of trade policy that forces members of Congress to delegate. He (Gilligan 1997, 6) points out, "after all Congress did not delegate to the president the power to set any trade policy, only to reduce trade barriers *reciprocally* with other countries" (original emphasis).

This point explains not only why legislators chose to delegate "over some other remedy to the universalistic logroll" (Gilligan 1997, 10), but also why legislators required positive congressional approval on trade agreements once fast-track procedures were adopted for the first time in the Trade Act of 1974. As argued above, Congress is very careful to ensure that the trade actions taken by the president are in line with legislators' preferences. It is no accident, therefore, that at the same time Congress expanded the president's negotiating authority to include non-tariff barriers, it reserved for itself a requirement of positive congressional approval of any negotiated trade agreement. In short, because the policy area is broad, we expect Congress to delegate only if it has to and to restrict that delegation of authority as much as possible. What we see is exactly that pattern of behavior.

Proposition III. Political Time

There are at least two ways in which the particular moment in political time offered opportunities and constraints that led to the enactment of NAFTA. A first point has to do with the emergence of an elite consensus on trade policy. Michael Gilligan points to a variety of trends in the second half of the twentieth century that made it more politically profitable for legislators to vote for free trade. He argues that the global economy is ever more interdependent, that American foreign policy increasingly came to be dominated by the search for export markets, and that the rise of the cold war meant that trade concessions would be used to stabilize economies in friendly nations (Gilligan 1997, 11). Gilligan also argues that an increasingly powerful export lobby began competing with the groups lobbying for protection of their industries so that the interest group playing field became, relatively speaking, more level. The result of all this was that free trade as an idea became a dominant political force. In particular, by the late 1980s, when legislators began considering trade barriers with Mexico, there "was a growing sense that trade barriers must be relaxed" (*Congressional Quarterly* 1990, 148). In his longitudinal study of a variety of policy areas, Gary Mucciaroni found that despite increased global competition and a breakdown of the pre-1970s free trade coalition, "protectionism's advance has been contained," both because of favorable institutional arrangements and "an intellectual commitment to liberal trade" (Mucciaroni 1995, 105–6). He concludes, "free trade remains a cherished (albeit tarnished) ideal among policy experts and top policymakers while protectionism remains discredited" (1995, 96). Indeed, in his research on trade policy in the 1980s, Pietro Nivola found that legislators who opposed free-trade initiatives felt positively ostracized. Nivola reported that one legislator who voted against the extension of fast-track authority in 1991 felt that,

voting against free trade was scorned as "not looking out for this country's interest." It is "almost a shameful thing," he concluded, "to be
labeled a protectionist." That agreeable generalization may not last for-
ever, but neither should it be dismissed as prematurely passe. (Nivola
1993, 149)

In addition to the fact that free trade as an idea had become popular, the
particular procedures utilized to enact NAFTA were also a result of prior
institutional evolution and development. As was discussed earlier, the concept of the congressional-executive agreement as a method of enacting international agreements was a relatively new innovation. Ackerman and Golove
(1995, 60) argue that NAFTA would likely not have been enacted if it had
been submitted as a treaty and that "if NAFTA had been negotiated in 1937,
Roosevelt would have submitted it as a treaty to the Senate without recognizing that he had a choice in the matter."

Fast-track procedures were also necessary because it was being enacted
by a particularly decentralized Congress. Nivola argues that by the mid-
1980s,

> access points in Congress abounded. Responsibility for managing trade
> had once been concentrated in the Senate Finance and House Ways and
> Means committees by virtue of their primary jurisdiction over tariffs. As
> trade questions moved beyond tariffs and conceptions of malfeasance
> changed, however, legislative power flowed downward to subcommittees
> and outward to other panels. At one time the chairmen of the two tax-
> writing committees could control the contents of trade bills. Now the cast
> of characters and the agendas they were trying to advance were becom-
> ing longer because of new, more complicated policy requirements and
> because of increased staff support and opportunities for political aggran-
> dizement. Participation spread to include the House Energy and
> Commerce Committee (domestic content, certification standards), the
> House Foreign Affairs and Senate Foreign Relations committees (foreign
> loans, export controls), the Judiciary committees (antitrust reciprocity),
> the banking committees (financial services, foreign investment, the
> Export-Import Bank), the agriculture committees (farm trade), the armed
> services committees (procurement codes), and so forth. Trade bills had
> always been potential legislative Christmas trees, but weaker congres-
> sional gatekeepers, multiple referrals, and new parliamentary norms that
> invited changes from the floor meant that more ornaments could be hung
> on them. (Nivola 1993, 97–99)

As a result, in addition to "regulating unfair trade," as a substitute for legis-lating, members of Congress retired to the relative safety and predictability of fast-track procedures. There, even at this decentralized moment in the institution's history, members of Congress could have input on the substance of a free-trade agreement, have the formal power to accept or reject the agreement, and keep the enabling legislation from dying a death of a thou-sand pinpricks.

Proposition IV. Existence of Powerful Champions

Another factor explaining the unusual tailor-made procedural choice in the case of NAFTA was the existence and institutional placement of powerful champions within the routine legislative process. As discussed earlier, leaders in both parties had essentially given the rank and file the option of tending to local concerns in the NAFTA vote. Nevertheless, it should not be over-looked that, in the end, each of the chamber's Democratic and Republican leaders supported NAFTA.[11] While the unanimous support of these leaders was important in terms of the signal that was sent to the rank and file, it was perhaps more important in terms of the signal it sent regarding side deals cut between individual legislators and President Clinton for their support. Members of Congress could vote for the package with the confidence their party leadership would sign on to whatever side deal required later ratifica-tion.

The vote to approve the enabling legislation for NAFTA also had the very active support of America's chief legislator—the president. While presidents also supported base closure, the Yucca Mountain Project, and, as we will see, tax reform, NAFTA required a level of involvement and support in the leg-islative process by the president that the others did not. Hook (1993, 3014) noted that, "this is not the kind of issue that can be won by appealing to vot-ing blocs. Every vote is being won and lost by intense, person-by-person per-suasion." That one-vote-at-a-time effort was undertaken by a White House determined to use "all its political currency to spend in the bazaar of con-gressional vote-trading: Phone calls from the president. Visits to the White House. The undivided attention of Cabinet officials. Promises of Clinton's support in the 1994 elections" (Hook, 1993, 3014). On this latter point, as noted above, Clinton even promised to defend congressional Republicans in the 1994 elections if their stance on NAFTA was attacked by Democrats.[12]

This intense activity by the president raises another interesting point about the peculiar nature of the fast-track procedures used in the case of NAFTA. We discussed above the notion that these procedures allowed for greater congressional input earlier in the process than is commonly acknowledged. But this process also encourages a bridge between the Congress and the president that proves useful later in attempting to round up support for the enabling legislation. In other words, the particular tailor-made procedures used in trade policy allow not only for greater policy collaboration and negotiation but for a greater shared sense of ownership over the final policy product. The end result, hopefully in addition to good public policy, is a legislative vehicle that will invariably enjoy the support of the key leaders within the more routine legislative process.

Proposition V. The One, the Few, and the Many

The final proposition in our theory of procedural choice has to do with the number of particularistic groups enduring the policy pain. All other things being equal, members of Congress are more likely to employ an extra-congressional procedure when the number of groups incurring costs is greater. In the case of NAFTA, the number of groups potentially incurring costs is, relatively speaking, quite large. This is not nuclear waste site choice where one community will incur the bulk of the costs, nor is it even similar to military base closure where many, but still a minority, of districts will incur costs. In this case, most every member of Congress will face opposition from some combination of union workers, affected industries, and/or agricultural concerns worried about foreign competition. From the perspective of this proposition, then, the surprising finding, discussed above, that Congress delegated far less authority than is commonly understood, becomes even more curious.

One explanation for this apparent contradiction, however, is offered by Michael Gilligan (1997), who argues that legislators came to support greater trade liberalization in part because of the rising political influence of exporter groups. In other words, groups seeking protection from international competition and from unequal trade practices were not the only particularistic players in this game. The battle over NAFTA was not simply a case of general benefits and particularistic costs, but one of general *and* particularistic benefits squaring off against particularistic costs.

It is not surprising that in this light the fast-track procedures employed in enacting NAFTA inhabit a procedural "gray area" somewhere between what we would describe as "internal" and "extra-congressional." Legislators of all stripes found themselves cross-pressured by a variety of groups. In this context, they legitimately came to believe that the best procedural path was a mix of extra-congressional and internal procedures that would give them some opportunity to protect their most vital interests while also affording them an opportunity to get a final agreement that would deliver the general benefits.

Conclusion

The fact that Congress failed to grant fast-track authority to the president in the years immediately following the enactment of NAFTA is worthy of our attention.[13] Theories of American trade policymaking institutions that suggest presidents dominate trade policy or that interest groups control American trade policymaking fail to recall that the Constitution grants Congress the authority to regulate commerce with foreign nations. As Sharyn O'Halloran (1994, ix) points out, "this might seem to be a simple point, but most previous studies of trade policy have failed to recognize its significance." Michael Gilligan agrees with this revision of the conventional wisdom surrounding trade policy. Congress did not delegate, as presidential dominance theorists argue, to take itself out of the trade game. Rather the choice of institutional arrangements is seen by Gilligan as an assertion of congressional power. He (Gilligan 1997, 10) argues, "specifically, delegation did *not* insulate Congress from constituency pressures—instead it transformed those pressures to include a voice for liberalization from exporters." Even I. M. Destler (1998, 95), who argues that in enacting fast-track procedures "Congress has tied members' hands," nonetheless concedes that in order to continue liberalizing global trade in the future,

> there needs to be a close executive-congressional working relationship in support of open trade policy. Specifically, this means close ties and mutual responsiveness between USTR and the two key trade committees, Senate Finance and House Ways and Means. (Destler 1998, 101)

So even for Destler, in recent years, the president appears to be playing a lesser role in trade policymaking.

Thus, while this chapter began with what appeared to be a paradox, it has ended with a greater confidence in the theory this study seeks to advance. At the beginning of this chapter, we asked why Congress would delegate authority in the case of NAFTA—a broad policy area in which particularistic costs are relatively geographically dispersed. We have seen that the key to answering this question is threefold. First, legislators delegated far less power to the president than is commonly understood. Congress constructed elaborate fire-alarm oversight mechanisms, provided itself with numerous opportunities to make legislator preferences clear to negotiators, and required that positive congressional action must be taken for any agreement to take effect. Second, legislators were able to pick and choose which particularistic interests required protection. Where particularistic benefits were geographically concentrated, and therefore more sensitive to legislators, legislators made sure they were capable of protecting their interests. Finally, there is some evidence that, to the extent legislators did delegate authority, they did so because they were seeking foreign trade concessions and this required executive negotiation. In short, as this study has hypothesized, rather than evading responsibility through delegation, the institutional mechanism Congress adopted to overcome the particular collective-action problem involved in NAFTA is far more a congressional triumph than an abdication.

FIVE

Tax Reform

In many ways, it is useful to think of the Tax Reform Act of 1986 (Public Law 99–514) as the mirror image of base closure. Base closure was a case where legislators imposed geographically concentrated costs in a narrow policy area while, in tax reform, legislators were operating in a broad policy area and taking away particularistic benefits that were (relatively speaking) geographically dispersed. It is not surprising to us, then, that in enacting these particularistic cuts in tax reform, Congress utilized its own internal procedures to get the job done. But, as we will see, procedural choice in tax reform, as in the case of base closure, was a function of more than just geography and the scope of the policy area. It was very much impacted by the moment in political time, the presence of powerful champions of the cause of tax reform, and the number and variety of groups that would endure the particularistic pain.

Before addressing the question of procedural choice, it is first necessary for us to understand the policy problem the legislative proponents of tax reform were attempting to address. After a very brief history of tax policy, we will examine the problem of tax reform and assess why so many believed the Tax Reform Act of 1986 (TRA86) would never become law. Finally, we will discuss the procedures utilized to pass TRA86 and devote some attention to each of the factors that impacted procedural choice.

A Brief History of the Income Tax

Foundations

The Constitution, written in 1787, did not give the national government clear authority to tax income. Article I, Section 8 did grant Congress the power "To lay and collect Taxes, Duties, Imposts and Excises, to pay the Debts and provide for the common Defence and general Welfare of the United States."

But the clause qualified that power, stating, "all Duties, Imposts and Excises shall be uniform throughout the United States." Article I, Section 9 added, "No capitation, or other direct, Tax shall be laid unless in Proportion to the Census or Enumeration herein before directed to be taken." As a result, while some income taxes were employed in very limited ways—mainly to address war-time deficits—the nineteenth century was primarily spent arguing over the constitutionality of the income tax. This debate culminated in the Supreme Court's 5–4 decision in 1895 that the income tax was a direct tax that hit certain states disproportionately and was therefore unconstitutional.

When the concept was given new life in 1913 with the adoption of a constitutional amendment, President Wilson and the Congress quickly enacted a very modest income tax that affected less than 2 percent of the population (Witte 1985, 78). From its modest beginnings, the income tax rapidly expanded with each successive political crisis in the first half of the twentieth century: World War I, The Great Depression, and World War II. More than any other event, however, the Second World War transformed the income tax from a tax on the wealthy to one that impacted most Americans. Whereas, before the war, those with incomes under $3,000 paid about 10 percent of all income taxes, by 1948, they were paying half (Conlan, Wrightson, and Beam 1990, 18). From this point on, the income tax stood as a permanent and significant part of American life.

World War II–1974

Like the other policy areas discussed in this book, tax policy in the three decades following World War II was characterized by a sub-government type of politics. Timothy Conlan, Margaret Wrightson, and David Beam (1990, 18) point out that "details, not principles, were the focus of action" during this period:

> Impenetrably complex and often boring, the making of tax policy became the province of a closed elite of key legislators, executive leaders, and lobbyists whose actions were seldom challenged (or even closely inspected) by the public or its elected representatives. Indeed, for much of the post–World War period—from 1958 through 1974—tax legislation was closely guarded and controlled by a single individual, Wilbur Mills, the powerful chairman of the House Ways and Means Committee.

None of this is to say that there was no change in tax policy in these years. On the contrary, tax bills were regularly drafted and adopted and the face of taxation changed over time. For instance, between 1948 and 1974, the share of federal revenues from the corporate income tax fell from 25.6 percent to 21.0 percent while the share of federal revenues from the individual income tax increased from 51.0 percent to 64.6 percent (Advisory Commission on Intergovernmental Relations, 1984, 46).[1] The rapid economic growth the nation experienced in the 1950s and 1960s fueled the rapid expansion in the individual income tax. Because of the progressive rate structure of the individual income tax, more and more of the tax burden automatically shifted from corporations to individuals. As a result, the individual tax rose in comparison with the corporate tax because of so-called bracket creep. The income tax rates were not indexed to inflation; therefore, while incomes were rising, taxpayers were being pushed into higher tax brackets. This provided the federal government with automatic revenue increases. And these increased revenues came more from individuals than from corporations because while the corporate income tax also utilized a multi-bracketed system throughout this period, there were fewer brackets and most corporations paid at the same rate.

For our purposes, the most significant way in which the face of tax policy changed in the post-war period was the expansion of so-called tax expenditures. These are tax deductions, credits, or other preferential treatment given to specific kinds of income that result in revenue losses. They are commonly referred to as tax expenditures because they provide monetary benefits that could otherwise be provided by federal loans, guarantees, or expenditures. Because the growth of the economy and bracket creep offered legislators pain-free revenue increases, it also offered legislators opportunities to provide tax relief. In that context, the question then became what form tax relief would take and tax expenditures were the most attractive choice for several reasons. As Douglas Arnold (1990) points out in his discussion of tax policy, across-the-board rate reductions are less attractive to legislators because small rate reductions become very expensive very quickly and those who benefit rarely appreciate what has been done for them. On the other hand, tax expenditures are very much appreciated by the beneficiaries, cost far less than across-the-board rate reductions, and most often provide legislators with an opportunity to claim credit for some general benefit. For instance, the mortgage interest deduction allows legislators to claim credit for expanding the housing stock in the nation and lowering the cost of housing. In this sense, then, tax expenditures offer legislators the additional benefit of being able to advance policy goals that they may be unable to advance through costly direct expenditure programs that require legislative oversight and large bureaucracies.[2]

Table 5.1
The Growth of Tax Expenditures

Period	New Tax Expenditures	New Tax Expenditures / Year
1914-1945	29	.91
1945-1974	30	1.03
1975-1981	15	2.14

Source: Data compiled from a list of all tax expenditures in Witte (1985, 276–81).

Given the fact that legislators prefer to provide tax relief through tax expenditures, we should not be surprised to see that the expansion of tax expenditures has been a regular staple of the history of tax policy. As we can see in Table 5.1, between 1913, the year the income tax was adopted, and 1974, Congress created tax expenditures at a rate of about one tax expenditure per year.

This pace accelerated rapidly after 1974 for a variety of reasons that we will examine in the next section. The important point here is to get some sense of the magnitude of tax expenditures as instruments of tax policy. By 1975, the cost of these tax expenditures (measured as lost revenue) was $92.9 billion per year or 56.6 percent of total federal income tax receipts (Witte 1985, 292).

1975–1986

Even though tax expenditures totaled nearly $93 billion in 1975, it is important to note that this "hidden welfare state"[3] had been constructed during a period when the Ways and Means Committee served as a guardian of the treasury. But the institutional upheavals of the late 1960s and early 1970s made the Ways and Means Committee far less likely to serve that function after 1974. Just as changes in the incentive structure in Congress had opened the door to legislators seeking to protect bases in their districts in the late 1970s and early 1980s, legislators were also more free to enact tax expenditures in the late 1970s and early 1980s.

As outlined in Table 5.1, the pace of enacting new tax expenditures accelerated in the late 1970s. This acceleration is even more staggering when one looks at the cost. By 1982, tax expenditures cost over $253 billion or 73.5 percent of federal income tax receipts (Witte 1985, 292). By 1985, the Joint Committee on Taxation (1985, 22) estimated that the fiscal 1986 revenue loss from tax expenditures would be over $424 billion.

How did this happen? The central reasons are institutional. Sunshine reforms, rules changes, changes in the membership of the Ways and Means Committee, the declining influence of the Ways and Means Committee vis-à-vis the Senate Finance Committee, and high inflation all conspired to create an atmosphere more conducive to the expansion of tax expenditures. Douglas Arnold (1990, 202) argues, "if one assumes that legislators' motives for creating and expanding tax preferences were unchanged, then one must consider both means and opportunity. In both instances there were significant changes."

The reforms of the early 1970s that were designed to make Congress more open to scrutiny and to participation by junior members hit the Ways and Means Committee particularly hard. Ways and Means drew the fire of reformers mainly because it was one of the power committees in the House. It was forced to become larger, to hold open hearings, and to create subcommittees; it lost its role as the "committee on committees" as well as its standing closed rule on the House floor. In expanding the Committee and opening it up, more and more members were recruited who were less "safe" electorally. For obvious reasons, these legislators would then have greater incentive than Ways and Means members in the past to provide benefits to constituents in the form of tax expenditures. As if that were not enough, the powerful Chairman of Ways and Means, Wilbur Mills, eventually lost his chairmanship when his alcoholism and his relationship with a stripper became public knowledge (Mucciaroni 1995, 46).

It is easy to see how less prestige and influence in the chamber, less centralized power, more open hearings, and less restrictive rules on the House floor for Ways and Means gave all legislators enhanced means to provide expanded tax expenditures to constituents. With Ways and Means retreating from its traditional role as guardian of the treasury, the influence of the Senate Finance Committee was on the rise; and the Finance Committee had always been a more hospitable place for the expansion of tax expenditures. With its more collegial atmosphere and far less restrictive rules, the Senate is a more institutionally fertile ground for tax expenditures.

As these institutional reforms provided the means for expanded tax expenditures, the opportunity was furnished by the succession of tax relief bills that were a result of the changed issue context of tax policy in the late 1970s. High inflation pushed more and more taxpayers into higher tax brackets; Congress thus found itself with the additional revenue necessary to enact tax relief bills in 1975, 1976, 1977, 1978, and 1981 (Arnold 1990, 202).

Last, but not least, among the expansions in tax expenditures that grew out of the reforms of the 1970s was the 1981 Economic Recovery Tax Act

(ERTA)—the Christmas tree to end all Christmas trees. John Witte (1995, 235) argues that the ERTA "was historically in a category by itself." The new law indexed income tax brackets to inflation, taking away the automatic revenue increases to which legislators had become accustomed. More importantly for our purposes, ERTA expanded and added new tax expenditures that grew radically in a short time. Witte (1985, 233) estimated that the new tax expenditure provisions of ERTA alone cost the federal government nearly $14 billion in fiscal 1982 and over $29 billion by fiscal 1983.

By 1985, the lost revenue from tax expenditures had reached a peak. In that year, the Joint Committee on Taxation (1985, 22) estimated that the lost revenue from all tax expenditures between fiscal 1986 and fiscal 1990 would be over 2.5 trillion dollars. As a result, when Senator Bill Bradley (D-NJ) began pushing for tax reform in 1982, the intuitive appeal of the idea seemed clear. Legislators would be able to vote for a significant tax rate reduction in return for trimming a variety of tax expenditures. The problems confronting such a piece of legislation were many, however, and it is worth our attention to outline in some detail why experts on the history of the income tax such as John Witte would declare in 1985 that rather than attempt to reform the tax code, policymakers ought to set their sights on simply halting the further erosion of the tax base.

> The answer is not to reform the tax system or even to seek immediate policy remedies, but rather to alter the political process to prevent even further regression. The general goal should be, as Allen Schick has compellingly argued, to restore non-decision making—to change the politics of taxation so as to retard and stabilize change. Thus, the goal should be to seek not remedies but merely a remission from the malady. And that requires political, not policy, reform. (Witte 1985, 380)

Given this melancholy forecast, we ought to outline why Witte and virtually every other expert on tax policy argued that fundamental tax reform was an impossible dream.

The Problem Posed by Tax Reform

The collective-action problem posed by tax reform is one not unfamiliar to us at this point. In their detailed account of the triumph of tax reform, Jeffrey Birnbaum and Alan Murray offer a concise but complete description:

> The groups with an interest in the existing tax system were well-organ-

ized and ready to defend their breaks at a moment's notice; the populace who stood to benefit from lower rates was unorganized and diffuse. Furthermore, Congress was a slow and cumbersome institution that usually made only piecemeal, incremental changes. Tax reform proposed something very different: a radical revamping of the entire tax structure. There was a tremendous inertia in Congress that resisted any such sweeping change. (Birnbaum and Murray 1987, 13)

In this atmosphere, rank-and-file legislators could not be counted upon as likely allies. One member of the Ways and Means Committee, Representative Willis Gradison (R-OH) argued, "this will inevitably be an uphill fight. The potential winners are skeptical that Congress will ever enact reform and the potential losers are organizing."[4] Moreover, legislators also knew that taking benefits away from one group and conferring them on another, is a negative-sum game. A decade earlier, the former chairman of the Senate Finance Committee, Senator Russell Long (D-LA), articulated precisely this view:

When we proceed to shift the taxes around so that one set of taxpayers pays a lot more taxes and somebody else pays a lot less taxes, the people who benefit from it do not remember it very long. They tend to feel that it should have been that way all the time, and the people who are paying the additional taxes resent it very bitterly.[5]

In addition to the collective-action problem posed by tax reform, there was also the problem of history. Conlan, Wrightson, and Beam point out that among the obstacles facing advocates of tax reform was the "bitter historical experience" tax reformers had endured. As one of those non-believers, John Witte (1985, 380) summarized this view best:

There is nothing, absolutely nothing in the history or politics of the income tax that indicates that any of these schemes have the slightest hope of being enacted in the forms proposed. In fact, if the past is any guide, reform efforts . . . are very likely to aggravate the problem over the long run. (Conlan, Wrightson, and Beam 1990, 7)

Finally, there was the additional question of whether Congress had the institutional capacity at the particular moment in political time to pass such a radical piece of legislation. Randall Strahan (1990, 143) points out that one of the biggest puzzles in explaining tax reform is that, "the critical first step in enacting reform was successfully undertaken by the Ways and Means

Committee, whose power, autonomy, and centralized leadership had been major targets of the congressional reform movement of the 1970s."

Thus, if procedural mechanisms were necessarily central to any effort to pass tax reform—as is the premise of this study—there was reason to think that the very committee in which tax reform legislation would need to originate was incapable of employing them. For that reason, many believed that tax reform, and all of tax policy more generally, ought to be handed over to an independent commission responsible for raising revenue.[6]

Such arguments notwithstanding, an extra-congressional procedure, or any kind of delegation for that matter, would not be the route for tax reform. In the end, this complex policy problem was handled by Congress, utilizing its own internal procedures to shield legislators from electoral retribution when possible. Before discussing why Congress handled this matter internally, it is useful to review the provisions of TRA86 as it was eventually adopted so that we have a sense of the scope and direction of the policy involved.

The Provisions of the Tax Reform Act of 1986

The central provisions of TRA86 cut income tax rates for both individuals and corporations and eliminated or scaled back numerous tax expenditures. The point of the exercise was to enhance the horizontal equity[7] of the tax code, make the tax code less complicated, and pass a bill that was revenue neutral. While the new law did not treat all income and all tax breaks equally, it did succeed in significant measure in each of these areas. The key provisions are listed in Table 5.2 below.

One result of all these provisions was a dramatic decline in both the numbers of tax expenditures and the revenue lost as a result of tax expenditures. Fourteen tax expenditures were repealed—roughly the same as the total number of tax expenditures repealed between 1913 and 1985 (Sandford 1993, 133). In April 1985, the Joint Committee on Taxation (1985, 22) projected that the total revenue lost from tax expenditures in fiscal 1990 would be $597.9 billion. In the wake of TRA86, in February 1987, the Committee (1987, 17) estimated that the lost revenue from tax expenditures in fiscal 1990 would be $335.7 billion—a difference of $262.2 billion.

Precisely because of these base-broadening measures, the significant rate reductions that were part of TRA86 were not budget busters. The bill was revenue neutral, meaning that the total revenue gained and lost from all the provisions of TRA86 summed roughly to zero. And with the exception of the fact that TRA86 removed roughly six million poor Americans from the tax rolls (Conlan, Wrightson, and Beam 1990, 3), the bill was also distribution-

Table 5.2
Key Provisions of the Tax Reform Act of 1986

Reduced
- the number of individual tax rate brackets from 14 to 2
- individual tax rates from a maximum marginal rate of 50% to 28%
- corporate income tax rates from a maximum rate of 46% to 34%, wit h lower brackets at 15% and 25%

Increased
- the standard deduction (or old "zero bracket" amount) from $2,480 to $3,000 for single taxpayers and from $3,670 to $5,000 for married couples
- personal and dependency exemptions from $1,080 to $2,000 in 1989 a nd after
- and liberalized the earned income tax credit for low -income families with children
- taxes on unearned income in excess of $1,000 by children under age 14 by applying the parents' top rate
- the alternative minimum tax (AMT) by adding preference an d adjustment items and raising the rate to 21%
- corporate minimum taxes by creating an alternative minimum tax of 20%, with a $40,000 exemption, to replace the previous add -on minimum tax
- penalties for tax negligence and fraud

Repealed
- deductions for state and local sales taxes
- deductions for consumer interest (like credit card, auto, and student loans), with a phase-out through 1990
- the "marriage penalty" deduction for two -earner households
- the $50 tax credit for political contributions
- the exclusion of $100 dividend income
- income exemptions for many "private activity" municipal bonds
- provisions for income -averaging
- the 60% deduction for long -term capital gains, treating all capital gains (short - or long-term) as ordinary income
- the exclusion o f income from unemployment compensation benefits
- deductions for expenses of adopting a child
- the exclusion for most prizes and awards
- deductions for charitable contributions by non -itemizers
- deductions for educational travel
- extra personal exemptions for the elderly and blind
- deductions for the land -clearing expenses of farmers
- lower rates on the capital gains of corporations
- the investment tax credit (ITC) for business expenditures on machinery, automobiles, and other property placed into service a fter December 31, 1985

Limited or Modified
- deductions for medical and dental care to expenses over a 7.5% income floor, up from 5% under previous law

Source: Conlan, Wrightson, and Beam (1990, 4–5)

ally neutral across income classes. The most noticeable shift resulting from TRA86 was that corporate taxes increased by roughly $24 billion per year while taxes on individuals decreased by the same amount. Some 80 percent of Americans thus received a direct tax cut as a result of TRA86 while corporate income taxes rose by 40 percent (Arnold 1990, 215).

Procedures as Key

While the tax cut for individuals that was part of TRA86 suggests some of the appeal of tax reform to legislators, the larger question that focuses this study remains. The taxes to be paid by corporations—a class with significant organizational presence in Washington—were increased by $120 billion over five years so that legislators could give a $120 billion tax cut to a general, diffuse public. How does Congress approve policies that impose particularistic pain in favor of a general benefit? Chapters 2–4 prove the old aphorism that necessity is the mother of invention. In closing military bases, choosing a site for nuclear waste, and approving a free-trade agreement for North America, legislators created new and unique institutional forms. While tax reform certainly did not utilize an extra-congressional procedure or even any procedures unique to the particular piece of legislation, it should be pointed out that the tactful utilization of legislative procedures was no less central to the enactment of TRA86.

Despite this centrality, however, what is most surprising about the standard accounts of the passage of TRA86 is the extent to which the deft use of procedures is not even mentioned. In the epilogue to the most widely read account of TRA86, Birnbaum and Murray (1987, 285) ask, "what created this legislative miracle that defied all the lessons of political science, logic, and history?"[8] They offer some description of how tax reform passed, but fail to include procedural tactics explicitly or implicitly. Similarly, in the other popular book-length account of tax reform, Conlan, Wrightson, and Beam (1990, 85) argue that TRA86 made its way through the House by "a combination of leadership, cajolery, calculation, idealism, and luck." While these amorphous elements were all no doubt present, this view fails to recognize the degree to which procedural tactics altered the environment in which idealistic leaders could cajole, legislators could calculate, and luck could be utilized.

The procedural tactics utilized were many, but they revolved around a single goal: weakening the links in the causal chain between legislators' votes and the loss of group benefits. A first step in this direction was taken by the chairman of the House Ways and Means Committee, Dan Rostenkowski (D-IL). Despite sunshine reforms a decade earlier, Rostenkowski had returned to closed committee markup sessions in 1982 (Strahan 1990, 143–44). By 1985, when the committee was considering tax reform, the use of closed committee hearings was nothing unusual. When simply closing the doors proved to be insufficient protection from interest group influence,[9] Rostenkowski employed a second procedural tactic—delegating difficult decisions to small informal task forces within the committee. In the end, Rostenkowski employed twelve such task forces that included between five and seven members each (Conlan, Wrightson, and Beam 1990, 115). This not only gave rank-and-file members of the committee some greater attachment to and pride in the committee's ultimate product, it also took the most difficult decisions out of the formal hands of the committee, reducing the number of opportunities for legislators to save specific tax breaks. Of this procedural innovation, Rostenkowski claimed, "they would work out a project, report back with some pride of creation, and then help me defend it."[10]

On the House floor, procedures were no less important. The bill was given a modified closed rule that allowed only three amendments—a Republican substitute and two other minor amendments. Moreover, the rule only allowed for five hours of debate—a brief period given the broad scope of the legislation involved (Birnbaum and Murray 1987, 162). In employing each of these tactics, the strategy of coalition leaders of TRA86 in the House was clear. Procedures would be used to ensure that most legislators—even many of the legislators on the Ways and Means Committee—would be shielded from the opportunity to save their favored tax break. Finally, one additional procedural tactic employed on the House floor that helped to weaken the traceability chain occurred by accident. When the time came for a vote on the bill itself, House Speaker Tip O'Neill (D-MA) spoke in a rote manner, "All those in favor say aye, opposed no, the bill is passed."[11] Birnbaum and Murray (1987, 175) relate what happened next:

> He then looked to the Republican side of the chamber, expecting to see a Republican member rise and call for a roll call, but no one moved. The speaker banged his gavel, and it was done. The Republicans, in a moment of confusion, had missed their only opportunity. A few Republicans made a show of complaining that the speaker had gaveled too quickly, but any fair witness could see that the Republicans had simply made a mistake.

Thus, TRA86 passed through the House without a roll call vote. The result was that most of the members did not have to go on the record as for or against the bill at all.

The fact that a number of the procedural tools available to coalition leaders in the House are not available to coalition leaders in the Senate is reflected in the differential treatment that tax packages receive on the House and Senate floors. The formal powers given to the Speaker and the Rules Committee in the House allow coalition leaders to bring complex legislative packages to the floor without offering rank-and-file legislators an opportunity to amend. The Senate, on the other hand, has two important relative disadvantages. First, the rules of debate and the rules governing amendments are very relaxed in the Senate. As a result, the body is generally run by unanimous consent agreements. As the name implies, any one senator is generally free to offer amendments to any bill at any time. Second, Article I, Section 7 of the Constitution provides that, "All Bills for raising Revenue shall originate in the House of Representatives; but the Senate may propose or concur with Amendments as on other bills." Effectively, this means that by the time a bill gets to the Senate floor, it is the proverbial last train leaving the station and each senator is anxious to add their own caboose. The result of these two procedural differences is not surprising. John Witte (1985, 323) examined all revenue-losing and revenue-gaining tax provisions enacted into law between 1970 and 1981 and classified them by which institutional actor— the executive branch, the House, or the Senate—had originally proposed the provision. He found that the executive branch and the House displayed rough balance between revenue-losing and revenue-gaining provisions with respective ratios of 1.17 and 1.34. The Senate, on the other hand, weighed in at 4.24. Of ninety-seven tax provisions originating in the Senate, only seventeen increased revenue.

Despite this difficult institutional environment, coalition leaders in the Senate were able to utilize several procedural tactics to their advantage. The Finance Committee first attempted to mark up the bill in open sessions and, not surprisingly, the revenue loss was staggering. So the first procedural tactic utilized was to privately draft a new bill behind closed doors. Once the members of the committee were satisfied with the central components of the bill, members met to mark up the bill in open session, and the first decision the committee made was to agree that all subsequent amendments must be revenue-neutral. This agreement forced particularistic interests to face off against other particularistic interests rather than particularistic interests against the general interest. After only a few amendments, the committee approved the bill 20–0 (Arnold 1990, 221).

On the Senate floor, there is no doubt that it helped that Finance Committee Chairman Robert Packwood (R-OR) had built a bipartisan coalition of thirty-five senators who agreed to oppose all amendments, and had established another informal agreement among senators that amendments be revenue-neutral (Conlan, Wrightson, and Beam 1990, 179). But Packwood

also received procedural relief from a provision of the 1974 Congressional
Budget and Impoundment Control Act. Arnold explains the provision which

> allowed any senator to raise a point of order against the consideration of
> a measure that would decrease revenues if Congress had not yet adopted
> its annual budget resolution. Although this prohibition could be over-
> turned by a majority vote waiving the point of order, it was much easier
> to defend a procedural vote of this kind than it was to defend the subse-
> quent amendment restoring group benefits. Only one senator challenged
> the agreement by proposing an unbalanced amendment, but the Senate
> refused, 54 to 39, to allow its consideration. (Arnold 1990, 222 n59)

Two other interesting procedural tactics utilized on the Senate floor
deserve mention. First, TRA86 was one of the first bills ever to be considered
and enacted in full view of live television cameras. According to Birnbaum
and Murray (1987, 179), this had a significant impact on the Senate floor:
"Members were leery of appearing to obstruct reform. They feared that their
usual long harangues might look unseemly to the public. Few wanted to risk
appearing in full color on the evening news as a defender of the 'special interests.'"

Second, when an amendment to restore the tax credit for IRA contributions was sponsored by Senator Alfonse D'Amato (R-NY), coalition leaders
offered a symbolic "sense of the Senate" resolution that the IRA issue should
be revisited in conference. Support for the resolution cooled support for
D'Amato's amendment, which was narrowly defeated by a 51–48 margin
(Conlan, Wrightson, and Beam 1990, 181).

The bills that emerged from the House and the Senate were substantially
different and, given the sensitivity of many of the provisions, those differences raised the possibility that TRA86 could unravel in conference. Again,
procedural tactics were utilized to save the bill. Conlan, Wrightson, and
Beam argue,

> the TRA conference converted the sunshine reforms of the mid-1970s,
> which were intended to open up conference proceedings to press and
> public scrutiny for the first time, into one of the blackest legislative boxes
> ever seen on Capitol Hill. Only the two chairmen and their top staffs
> were present when most of the critical decisions were finally reached.
> Until they were called upon to ratify the agreements, most conferees
> seemed as far removed from the process as any Senate page. (Conlan,
> Wrightson, and Beam 1990, 190–91)

The way the conference was handled, and the presence there of the top staff from the Joint Committee on Taxation, raises one other important procedural point. Because writing tax legislation is such a fiercely technical task requiring complex revenue estimates from highly trained staff, those who control access to staff resources are in an advantaged position. As a result, because pro-reform Rostenkowski and Packwood had greater control over staff resources, they were able to frustrate the ability of anti-reform legislators even to propose amendments and alternatives.

It is clear, then, that despite the lack of systematic attention devoted to the deft utilization of procedures in the passage of TRA86, the bill could not have otherwise survived. Arnold sums up this view well:

> If legislators had not chosen to accept these extraordinary procedures in order to weaken the traceability chain for group effects, the electoral connection would have prevented many of them from ever supporting tax reform. There can be little doubt that these procedures were essential for tax reform. (Arnold 1990, 223)

Applying the Theory: Procedural Choice and Tax Reform

That procedures were central to the passage of TRA86 is thus clear. What is less clear is the answer to the question that consumes this study. Why those procedures? Why didn't legislators choose one of the several degrees of delegation that characterized each of the three previous cases? The answer to this question is to be found in examining the same factors that we looked at in those cases. Because of a variety of factors particular to the policy area and the policy instrument involved, legislators did not need to utilize an extra-congressional procedure. On the contrary, there is reason to believe that legislators wanted to handle TRA86 internally because the bill offered opportunities for claiming credit *as well as* avoiding blame for the loss of particularistic benefits.

Proposition I. Geographic Concentration of Costs

The first factor impacting procedural choice is the nature of the particularistic benefit being cut or the particularistic cost being imposed. Because he is one of the few authors who explicitly discusses the importance of the nature of the particularism involved, it is not surprising that Arnold (1990, 216) assesses the impact of the geographic distribution of particularistic cuts in tax

reform. He argues, "coalition leaders quickly learned that a reform bill needed to be geographically neutral in order to survive all the legislative hurdles."
Arnold continues,

> Although coalition leaders failed to terminate any major tax prefer-
> ences that were geographically concentrated, they were far more suc-
> cessful in eliminating those that were geographically dispersed.
> Legislators on the tax-writing committees could protect but a limited
> number of tax preferences without undermining the entire bill. They
> quite naturally chose to protect geographic benefits, lest they be
> accused of neglecting their constituents, while allowing coalition lead-
> ers to terminate dozens of group benefits that were geographically dis-
> persed. Many legislators may have wished to help the real estate,
> financial, and restaurant industries, but none had a powerful reason to
> demand protection for these industries as their price for supporting the
> whole bill. (Arnold 1990, 217)

Specifically, Arnold suggests that the relatively small price paid by the oil
and gas industry and the retention of the deductibility of state and local
income and property taxes are evidence of the privileged position of geographically concentrated benefits in the scramble to find tax expenditure
cuts to pay for lower tax rates. Aside from these general claims, however,
Arnold offers no empirical support for what is a central idea in the context
of this study. If it is true that legislators do care more about protecting geographically concentrated benefits than geographically dispersed ones, and if
they, in fact, did this in the case of tax reform, the nature of the particularistic benefit would go a long way toward explaining procedural choice.
While eliminating tax expenditures imposes both geographically concentrated and geographically dispersed costs on groups, Arnold is suggesting that
TRA86 was handled internally because legislators could selectively protect
the types of benefits that were most sensitive and thus minimize the electoral
damage. It is important, then, that we examine the differential treatment of
tax benefits with an eye toward geography to seek out evidence to support
or refute Arnold's claim.

While they don't always refer explicitly to the geographic concentration of
benefits, several authors argue that there is wide variation in the kinds of tax
expenditures that exist and that this variation matters. For instance, in
explaining that a significant portion of tax expenditures originates in the
executive branch, Christopher Howard suggests that members of Congress
are more likely to be partial to a certain kind of tax expenditure:

I find it more plausible that the reelection motive applies less to the creation of tax expenditures with social welfare objectives than it does to the
creation of other kinds of tax expenditures. This motive may become more
salient after the program has been created. Under conditions of fiscal
stress, members of the revenue committees may claim credit for keeping
existing tax expenditures off the chopping block. (Howard 1997, 186)

Similarly, James Buchanan points out the important distinction in political
logic between individual and corporate tax expenditures. He argues,

if individual taxpayers are presumed to be unable to trace out the inci-
dence and effects of alternative corporate tax structures, the observed
support for the 1986 tax law changes may have reflected a failure to
make the translation from corporate to individual tax accounts.
(Buchanan 1987, 31)

Describing the political environment in the House Ways and Means
Committee, Randall Strahan argues that there was a clear geographic pattern
to which tax expenditures were saved and which were not.

Rostenkowski was forced to shift from a coalition-building strategy stress-
ing opportunities for enhancing prestige and enacting good public policy
to a strategy that included negotiating changes to accommodate local or
group interests of importance to individual committee members. As one
committee member described the markup process, "There was an awful
lot of protection going on—in terms of protecting *what's good for your
state, your region, your district.*" By the count of a staffer who worked
closely with the chairman, five of the twenty-eight members of the coalition that ultimately supported the committee bill (four Democrats and one
Republican) supported the chairman from the outset; the remainder exact-
ed as a condition of support at least some concessions for *interests of local
or regional concern.* (emphasis added) (Strahan 1990, 149)

Finally, James Snyder Jr. makes the point more explicitly, arguing,

tax preferences for specific industries or firms, such as those for agriculture, timber, oil and gas, Philips Petroleum, and Cimarron Coal, clearly
have the properties of locally concentrated benefits and diffuse costs. On
the other hand, for many big-ticket, federal versus local tax policy issues—
such as the deductibility of state and local sales taxes and the deductibili-

ty of interest on state and local bonds—both benefits and costs are dispersed rather widely, at least viewed geographically. (Snyder 1993, 183)

In making this point, of course, Snyder leaves out state and local income and property taxes, the deductibility of which was retained in TRA86. We are left to assume that the reason legislators retained the deductibility of state and local income and property taxes while eliminating the deduction for state and local sales taxes was because the benefits of the deductibility of state and local income and property taxes are more geographically concentrated than the benefits of state and local sales tax deductibility. That is also the explanation to be inferred from Arnold's claim that state and local income and property tax deductibility were retained because of their geographically concentrated character.

Fortunately, this happens to be a case in which we can do more than infer from claims made by a number of authors. Data on per capita state and local taxes are readily available and serve as an excellent measure of the comparative concentration of the benefits of the deductibility of state and local sales, income, and property taxes. Because our hypothesis is that geographically concentrated benefits are more difficult for legislators to cut, we would expect to find that in choosing which tax preferences to retain and which to eliminate, legislators would retain those that are more geographically concentrated and eliminate those more geographically dispersed. In addition, we know that in TRA86, legislators retained the deductibility of state and local income and property taxes and eliminated the deductibility of state and local sales taxes. Therefore, if the geographic concentrations of these taxes are an important variable in determining which tax benefits are cut and which are spared, we should see some statistically significant difference between the variation in per capita state and local income and property taxes on the one hand and the variation in per capita state and local sales taxes on the other.

Table 5.3 provides comparative measures of variation between states for per capita state and local income, property, and sales taxes for both fiscal 1985 (right before the enactment of TRA86) and fiscal 1988 (right after the enactment of TRA86). As expected, we see that there is significantly greater variation among states in state and local per capita income and property taxes compared with per capita sales taxes. This greater variation means that the benefits of the deductibility are more geographically concentrated in certain states whose members then have a unique and significant incentive to retain the deductibility of these taxes.

Moreover, as we will see shortly, the drive to retain the deductibility of state and local income and property taxes came from the House. For this reason, it

Table 5.3

Comparative Variation between States of Per Capita State and Local Sales, Income, and Property Taxes

	Fiscal 1985	Fiscal 1988
Std. Deviation of Per Capita Sales Tax in 50 States	$156.40	$175.66
Std. Deviation of Per Capita Income Ta x in 50 States	$195.75	$235.63
Std. Deviation of Per Capita Property Tax in 50 States	$212.47	$240.38
F Statistic for Income Tax versus Sales Tax	1.566*	1.799**
F Statistic for Property Tax versus Sales Tax	1.845**	1.873**

Source: Statistics above are from author's calculations based on data from Tax Foundation (1988, Table 31) and Tax Foundation (1991, Table 31).
* Significant at .1
** Significant at .05

is appropriate to weight the state per capita tax payments in Table 5.3 by the number of House members from each state. The results of this weighting are displayed in Table 5.4. We can see there that the disparity between sales taxes and income and property taxes becomes even greater.

In addition to this empirical evidence, there is more than ample anecdotal evidence to suggest that geography played a significant role in explaining why income and property tax deductibility was retained while sales tax deductibility was eliminated. For instance, Conlan, Wrightson, and Beam (1990, 95) point out that the state and local income tax deduction was a particularly difficult provision for legislators to eliminate because "such popular provisions were not viewed by the average taxpayer as special-interest loopholes. They were often incidental *to where one worked or lived,* and few used the provisions as a ploy to lower taxes" (emphasis added).

This fact and the high concentration of benefits from deductibility of state and local income and property taxes were not lost on the members of the House. In the Ways and Means Committee, where three committee members were from New York—the state with the highest per capita state income tax in the nation—retaining the state and local income and property tax deduction became "the fulcrum of reform" (Conlan, Wrightson, and Beam 1990, 112). In addition to the influence of committee members from high-tax states, Speaker Tip O'Neill (D-MA) made it clear to Chairman Rostenkowski that eliminating the state and local income and property tax deduction was unacceptable: "Dan, the power of the Speaker comes down to whether a bill gets on the floor or doesn't get on the floor. Two things I'm interested in: state

Table 5.4

Comparative Weighted Variation between States of Per Capita State and Local Sales, Income, and Property Taxes

	Fiscal 1985	Fiscal 1988
Std. Deviation of Per Capita Sales Tax in 50 States	$114.44	$131.77
Std. Deviation of Per Capita Income Tax in 50 States	$230.87	$284.88
Std. Deviation of Per Capita Property Tax in 50 States	$162.37	$199.27
F Statistic for Income Tax versus Sales Tax	4.070*	4.674*
F Statistic for Property Tax versus Sales Tax	2.013*	2.287*

Source: Statistics above are from author's calculations based on data from Tax Foundation (1988, Table 31) and Tax Foundation (1991, Table 31).
* Significant at .0001

and local taxes. You don't have those in the bill, you don't get a day in the court. Remember that."[12]

The fate of the state and local sales tax deduction in the Senate provides further evidence of the importance of the geographic concentration of particularistic benefits. Looking back at Tables 5.3 and 5.4, we are not surprised that when the House version of tax reform allowed the state and local sales tax deduction to be eliminated, there would be a move in the Senate to reinstate it. The variation in per capita state and local sales tax is significantly lower when the data are weighted by the number of members in the House from each state, indicating that benefits of retaining the state and local sales tax deduction were more likely to be sensitive to members of the Senate than members of the House. Senators David Durenberger (R-MN) and Daniel Patrick Moynihan (D-NY) wanted to restore the deduction on the Senate floor, but because retaining the deduction would blow a $17.5 billion hole in the bill, and because most senators were committed to revenue neutrality on all amendments, neither senator was willing to put forward an amendment. When several other senators put forward an amendment that would allow taxpayers to deduct either their state sales tax or their income taxes, but not both, senators from high-income tax states turned against the deductibility of state and local sales taxes for fear that the amendment would open up the possibility of tampering with state income tax deductibility in conference (Conlan, Wrightson, and Beam 1990, 183–84). Highlighting the different political calculus for the sales tax vis-à-vis income and property taxes, Moynihan would later explain his reversal by pointing out, "the sales tax was no big deal for New York."[13]

In addition to the state and local tax deductions, the other set of geographically concentrated tax expenditures mentioned by Arnold were tax preferences for the oil and gas industry. Just as retention of the state and local income and property tax deductions were critical components of passing tax reform in the House, the retention of oil and gas tax credits was critical in the Senate. Despite the lack of a strong oil and gas presence on Ways and Means, the warning signs on this geographic benefit were clear at the House Committee stage when lawmakers from oil and gas states voted in lock step to retain the deduction for state and local income and property taxes. Birnbaum and Murray point out that,

> Rostenkowski's people knew there was trouble for sure when Democratic Representative James Jones of Oklahoma wrote an op-ed piece for *The Washington Post* that demanded the retention of the deduction for state and local taxes. State taxes in Oklahoma were so low that President Reagan had chosen Jones's home state to make his biggest pitch for repeal of that deduction. He argued the write-off represented a subsidy by low-tax states like Oklahoma to high-tax states like New York, but Jones wasn't buying that line. For political expediency, Jones and other "oilies" had joined forces with New York Jewish groups to protect each other's tax breaks. (Birnbaum and Murray 1987, 129)

The Senate Finance Committee, in particular, proved to be a hostile environment for cutting oil and gas tax expenditures. When Chairman Packwood brought the bill to committee, he quickly met resistance.

> The committee rank-and-file promised nothing but trouble. Building on a bloc of oil and gas votes that included Long, Dole, Bentsen, Max Baucus, D-Mont., and Malcolm Wallop, R-Wyo., outspoken opponent David Boren, D-Okla., was actively soliciting conspirators for his "kill the bill" coalition. (Conlan, Wrightson, and Beam 1990, 148)

The truth is, however, that this assessment actually understates the role that oil and gas would play in the Finance Committee. Before the bill had ever been sent to Congress from the Treasury Department, oil and gas interests, led by Secretary of the Treasury James Baker, a Texan, had been successful in removing provisions from the bill that would have taken some $44 billion in tax benefits from the oil and gas industry over five years. Given the differing geographic makeup of the House in general, and the Ways and Means Committee in particular, it is not surprising that oil and gas interests

Table 5.5.
Comparison of Dependence on Oil and Gas Extraction by State

Senator	% of State's 1986 GSP from Oil and Gas Extraction	State Rank
Long (D-LA)	17.90%	2
Wallop (R-WY)	17.35%	3
Boren (D-OK)	8.85%	4
Bentsen (D-TX)	8.25%	5
Baucus (D-MT)	3.02%	8
Dole (R-KS)	2.06%	11
Armstrong (R-CO)	1.62%	12
Pryor (D-AR)	1.08%	14
Heinz (R-PA)	0.18%	20
Moynihan (D-NY)	0.08%	27
Symms (R-ID)	0.04%	29
Durenberger (R-MN)	0.03%	30
Roth (R-DE)	0.01%	34
Packwood (R-OR)	0.01%	35
Danforth (R-MO)	0.01%	36
Chafee (R-RI)	0.01%	40
Mitchell (D-ME)	0.01%	41
Grassley (R-IA)	0.00%	43
Matsunaga (D-HI)	0.00%	44
Bradley (D-NJ)	0.00%	45

Oil and Gas Extraction as % of Gross National Product	1.06%
Oil and Gas Extraction as % of Finance Committee Member States' GSP	2.89%

Source: Author's calculations of data from Bureau of Economic Analysis, U.S. Bureau of the Census

had been hit. But the partisan and geographic makeup of the Senate and the Senate Finance Committee were far more hospitable to oil and gas interests. First, the Senate had a Republican majority more sympathetic to Baker's political logic, and the bias of that logic was clear. One anonymous administration official was quoted in the *National Journal* as saying of the offending oil and gas provisions, "the Republican party is going to have to find a new way to finance campaigns in Texas if this goes through."[14]

Administration influence notwithstanding, a second and more important reason why oil and gas tax expenditures would receive favorable treatment in the Finance Committee had to do with the geographic makeup of the committee. Table 5.5 displays the percentage of the gross state product comprised by oil and gas extraction for each state represented on the Senate Finance Committee. Eight of the fourteen states with the largest oil and gas sectors are represented on the Finance Committee, including numbers 2 through 5. Overall, the twenty states represented on Finance derive nearly three times as much of their economies from oil and gas extraction as compared with the United States as a whole.

For the purposes of this study, however, this latter statistic is less important than the former. The existence of a solid bipartisan minority of senators intensely committed to preserving oil and gas tax benefits meant that tax reform could proceed through Finance only when this geographically concentrated interest was appeased. Conlan, Wrightson, and Beam point out that on the final day of committee markup, when it was becoming clear that the proverbial train would be leaving the station, the oil and gas bloc was more successful than any other group. They add,

> The outcome was only a matter of who had the votes. In the end it was not Packwood, and so energy-state senators won their amendments to protect tax benefits enjoyed by "working interests" in oil and gas projects. Like others, Boren owed his committee assignment to Long, and all had profited handily from the alliance. It was a nonideological, nonpartisan marriage of convenience that no one, not even Wallop, was about to abandon, tax reform or no tax reform. Energy's strong track record, in turn, was enough to convince the core group that, without an accommodation, the committee might be unable to report a bill. It shows that, even during a period of remarkable esprit de corps, traditional alliances never wholly broke down. (Conlan, Wrightson, and Beam 1990, 176)

Significantly, the battle lines over the oil and gas amendments show how the power of geography can overwhelm the power of party. Dole (R-KS), Bentsen (D-TX), Boren (D-OK), and Long (D-LA) fought and won on oil and gas against Chafee (R-RI), Bradley (D-NJ), and Mitchell (D-ME).

In addition to the special treatment accorded the oil and gas industry and state and local tax deductions, the important role of transition rules in enacting TRA86 serves as further evidence of the importance of geography. Technically, transition rules are special provisions inserted into tax bills that provide for an easier transition between old tax law and new. But because the chairmen of Finance and Ways and Means have effective control over who gets transition rules, it is easy to see how these provisions are the grease that lubricates the legislative tax machine. And because transition rules are targeted toward specific companies or localities, they are perhaps the purest form of a geographic benefit. The best-case scenario for legislators seeking to protect constituency interests in tax reform would be to save the tax expenditures their constituents utilize most. A second-best scenario is to get a favorable transition rule that will ease the loss of the tax benefit. In the case of tax reform, transition rules were used to help move the bill over each legislative hurdle.

During the markup of TRA86 in the Ways and Means Committee, Chairman Rostenkowski, sensing he was about to lose revenue to an amendment that would expand the deductibility of business lunches, pleaded with the committee that the deduction should be scaled back as a matter of fairness. But he also pointed out that there would be a bill, and that he would decide who got transition rules and who did not. Birnbaum and Murray (1987, 146) describe what followed. "Rostenkowski's threat to deny transition rules to any member who crossed him could not be ignored. Whether it was Rostenkowski's plea for reform or his threat to deny transition rules that caused the change, the committee majority shifted after the speech."

On the final day of markup, Rostenkowski did indeed dispense more than $5 billion in transition rules to members who had been friendly or to those who the Chairman hoped would still be willing to get on board. Not surprisingly, Rostenkowski also inserted a number of favorable transition rules for Representative Claude Pepper (D-FL), the chairman of the House Rules Committee, whom Rostenkowski knew he would need to get a favorable rule for the bill on the House floor (Birnbaum and Murray 1987, 146–47).

Transition rules were no less a part of the success Chairman Packwood had in the Finance Committee (Mucciaroni 1995, 52). As one participant in the final moments in Finance relates, the hunt for transition rules sometimes looked like the floor of a stock exchange.

> Packwood was standing up there talking like an auctioneer: "I've got fifty [million] here. Can I take fifty [million] there?" Overall, that's what it came down to. He was holding up this paper and auctioning off provisions in order to pay for the last few special deals.[15]

On the Senate floor, Packwood's control over transition rules also helped to keep troops in line. After Senators Pete Wilson (R-CA) and Alan Cranston (D-CA) had abandoned the chairman on an amendment seeking to expand tax credits for contributions to IRAs—an amendment Packwood had beaten back by the slimmest of margins—Packwood got behind an amendment by Senator Howard Metzenbaum (D-OH) to eliminate a transition rule for Unocal that California's senators had requested. When the amendment passed by a wide margin, the message to other senators was clear (Conlan, Wrightson, and Beam 1990, 185).

In conference, transition rules emerged again as a saving grease. When trouble broke out among Senate conferees, Packwood made a point of reminding his fellow conferees that he and Rostenkowski would each have about $3 billion in additional transition rules to hand out and that those who supported the conference report would be remembered. Some were remembered more quickly than others, as Senator Chafee (R-RI) dropped his objections after Packwood provided Rhode Island $100 million in authority to issue certain types of tax-free bonds (Birnbaum and Murray 1987, 277–79). In its final version, TRA86 contained nearly seven hundred transition rules at a total cost of $11 billion—every one of them a geographically concentrated benefit for some member of Congress (Arnold 1990, 218).

In concluding our discussion of the geographic concentration of costs, it is important to be reminded of our focus—procedural choice. It is clear that legislators were willing and able to utilize an internal procedural strategy in the case of TRA86 precisely because it allowed them to make the very choices we have discussed in the preceding pages. Summarizing the final contours of the bill, Conlan, Wrightson, and Beam offer this revealing passage:

> The TRA is neither pluralist in tone nor modest in the scope of its departure from its predecessor, and interest-group bargaining was clearly not the dominant influence on the legislation. Indeed, losers constituted a virtual *Who's Who* among the U.S. economic interests that traditionally have shaped tax policy, including real estate, heavy industry, large banks, casualty insurance, defense contractors, and multinational corporations. (Conlan, Wrightson, and Beam 1990, 233–34)

Noticeably absent from this list, however, were beneficiaries of geographically concentrated tax expenditures. Legislators proceeded with tax reform precisely because they employed a procedure that allowed them to choose winners and losers. Senator Russell Long (D-LA) expressed this view best in defending the oil and gas interests so vital to his state against an amendment supported by a former judge, Senator George Mitchell (D-ME), who argued for "blind justice" in tax reform.

> We fellas are lawmakers. We're supposed to know who we're helping and do it deliberately and know who we're hurting and do that deliberately. Now, the people in the oil and gas business are the most depressed industry in the United States. If you're sitting over there in court, I can under-

stand your saying, "I'm blindfolded. I'm going to treat them all the same. This fella's broke, down and out. God knows he needs help. But, the hell with him. I can't do anything about that." If you're a judge, that's how you do it. If you're a lawmaker, you'd say, "That poor fella needs help. Let's help him."[16]

Not surprisingly, the tax expenditures most legislators sought to save were the most sensitive particularistic benefits of all—geographically concentrated benefits.

Proposition II. Scope of the Policy Area

Tax reform is arguably the most broad of the policy areas discussed in this book. TRA86 not only put every aspect of the then nearly $500 billion in revenue from individual and corporate income taxes on the table, but also touched upon and affected virtually every other policy area. Conlan, Wrightson, and Beam (1990, 230) correctly point out that TRA86 is an interesting story for students of American politics if only because of "the size and sweep of the TRA, bringing nearly every important institution and interest in national politics to the foreground." Birnbaum and Murray make the point more explicitly, suggesting that tax reform was fundamentally different from dealing with more narrow policy areas. Early on, Treasury Secretary James Baker and his lieutenant, Richard Darman, had hoped to secretly cut a deal with key legislators ahead of time and push tax reform through the Congress just as they had done with Social Security in 1983. But Birnbaum and Murray (1990, 76) argue such a strategy could never have worked in the case of tax reform because "rewriting the nation's tax code was far more complex than propping up a single program like Social Security. The tentacles of the tax system reached into every area of American life; lawmakers were not likely to rubber stamp such a far-reaching set of proposals."

Enacting tax reform thus poses more legislative problems than just cutting visible and concentrated particularistic benefits in favor of a diffuse general benefit. It also means making decisions in other policy areas in which legislators and citizens have cross-cutting policy preferences. In relating some of the difficulties encountered while negotiating the final contours of TRA86 in conference, Conlan, Wrightson, and Beam provide two examples of this problem:

> Not only did conferees despair over changes affecting most corporations, they also dug in on narrow policy and constituent concerns. For example, Bill Roth—an advocate of savings incentives and a consumption tax

to discourage spending—made IRAs his line in the sand. When Packwood went back on his promise (made earlier during Senate floor debate) to help Roth out in conference, the Republican from Delaware withheld his support. Similarly, Danforth was determined to preserve the so-called completed contract method of accounting for defense contractors. When he couldn't, this much-respected Presbyterian minister voted against the conference agreement and, later, against the TRA. (Conlan, Wrightson, and Beam 1990, 210–11)

Thus, while legislators wanted to protect the particular benefits flowing to their districts, tax reform's broad scope added an additional dimension of complexity. Legislators could be sure in the case of base closure that the agency losses incurred by delegating authority to draw up a list of bases to be closed would be limited. But in the case of tax reform, legislators could conceivably lose particularistic tax benefits *and* lose in a host of other policy areas far beyond the tax code. The power to tax, after all, is the power to destroy. Given these facts, it is inconceivable that legislators could feel secure delegating any power to reform the tax code. The institutional prerogatives at stake were made clear in Rostenkowski's response to Baker's plan to move TRA86 through the Congress quickly. He recalls,

I sat in my rocker and said: "Jesus, Jim, don't show me how imprudent you are! You are viewing this as though we are going to a conference. We're creating legislation, and this is the first step in the process. We're going to have hearings. I'm going to take testimony. This will take us at least a year—or two."[17]

While the concern over agency losses would certainly be enough to prevent legislators from delegating the power to craft tax reform to a base closure type of commission, the case of tax reform also points out a second, and perhaps more compelling, reason why legislators are unlikely to delegate authority in broad policy areas. Precisely because the particular laws we are focusing on in this study confer general benefits that are diffuse while they impose concentrated costs, we expect legislators to want to delegate the authority to make these decisions so long as they can contain agency losses. But TRA86 presents such a massive policy area that delivering the diffuse general benefit actually offers legislators some positive political reward.

This differs from cases like base closure and nuclear waste in a fundamental way. In these cases, legislators can support the policy vehicle when, and only when, they are reasonably sure that the electoral fallout from their vote will be negligible. Importantly, we did not see legislators lining up to take credit for base closure or the siting of a nuclear waste repository. The reason for this is that the general benefits delivered in these narrow policy areas are so small, indirect, and difficult to detect, that claiming credit for them is neither useful nor credible.

TRA86, on the other hand, because of its size and scope, offers legislators an opportunity to claim credit for delivering a significant benefit. Arnold summarizes the logic well:

> Coalition leaders quickly discovered that comprehensive tax reform was easier to achieve than incremental reform. Whereas a proposal to elimi-nate or reduce a few tax preferences could offer only imperceptible gener-al benefits, such as a minor rate reduction or a modest revenue increase, comprehensive reform offered dramatically lower rates that everyone could appreciate. This fact helped transform the politics of the situation. Rather than pitting a few groups with a great deal at stake against an indifferent general public with virtually nothing at stake, the new plan forced people to consider whether they were better off with high rates and lots of loopholes or with lower rates and fewer loopholes. The new lower rates became the principal attraction of tax reform. (Arnold 1990, 213)

With legislators thus focused on the general benefit and on the opportunity to claim credit, the normal political logic went out the window. For instance, while the normal course of events in a conference committee on a tax bill was to combine the pet loopholes of both sides, the conferees in TRA86 sought to combine the loophole-*closing* provisions from both the House and the Senate to get rates down as low as possible. Quite often, as a result, confer-ees chose the tougher provision from the House and Senate bills for the final version of TRA86.[18]

Coalition leaders were so successful in putting the general benefit up front that, ultimately, many legislators came to believe that they had to vote for TRA86 lest they incur the wrath of angry constituents. Conlan, Wrightson, and Beam (1990, 174) correctly point out, "to be sure, directing blame or credit for tax reform was not at that time on the minds of average Americans." But what really matters most to legislators is their perception of what average Americans will be thinking, or what they might be made to think, on Election Day. Mucciaroni argues,

> members of Congress who might have been tempted to vote against reform risked having challengers at the next election point out that they

had denied their constituents a diffuse benefit and that they were captives of privileged interests. In other words, their opponents could assert that they had had the opportunity to vote for greater fairness and efficiency and less government, and they had shied away from it. In the end their fear and the media glare that attended their vote compelled many members to support reform. (Mucciaroni 1995, 38–39)

More than anyone, legislative leaders feared being blamed for failing to enact TRA86. One senior Ways and Means Committee aide recalled,

when we had trouble, when we lost on the bank vote, . . . [the chairman's] argument tended to be: "We can't do this. The Democrats are going to get blamed for killing tax reform. I can hear Ronald Reagan out there right now saying your rates are now 50 [percent] and I could have lowered them to 35 [percent]."[19]

That legislative leaders had these sorts of worries was important. In his analysis of the enactment of TRA86, James Buchanan (1987, 33) suggests the possibility that tax reform was promoted "by political entrepreneurship of self-interested agents who exploited the temporary coincidence between their own and general constituency interests."

This view assigns too passive a role to legislative leaders, however. Legislative leaders, as we have seen, actively manipulated procedures, and the legislation itself, to create an atmosphere in which the general benefit of tax reform was put up front. For instance, the final bill gave individuals a net tax cut of roughly $24 billion annually and increased corporate taxes by the same amount. The benefits of this tax cut were spread around so that 80 percent of Americans would pay less in taxes—an average of 6.1 percent less to be exact (Arnold 1990, 214–15). Individuals file tax returns every year and are likely to notice a difference of this size. Though corporate tax increases are eventually passed on to individuals in the form of lower corporate earnings, lower dividends, increased prices, or reduced services, these costs are indirect and difficult for voters to trace to the actions of legislators.

Moreover, legislative leaders did more than spread the general benefit around. Once again, they manipulated the procedures they could, utilizing the newly installed Senate television cameras to shame senators pushing for amendments that were not revenue-neutral or that disproportionately favored wealthier individuals or corporations. When Senator Alfonse D'Amato (R-NY) and Senator Christopher Dodd (D-CT) sought to restore some of the deduction for contributions to IRAs, Senator Bill Bradley (D-NJ) came to the floor with charts to explain how the amendment would benefit only wealthy taxpayers. Bradley's tax aice, Gina Despres, pointed out the utility of the cameras:

> Television was just fortuitous and terrific, providing an opportunity to make the general interest real. The general interest could be portrayed as the little man trying to crawl out of a hole. For each amendment, we could point to this little guy and show that he would get zip while the guy making $200,000 would make out like a bandit. This was show biz.[20]

Procedures and modifications of the bill aside, the point for our purposes is that the general benefit was large enough that legislators had a positive incentive to support tax reform. This could not have been the case in base closure or nuclear waste, as the general benefit was not large enough for legislators to credibly claim their actions had any positive impact on citizens' lives. Therefore, in addition to the fact that legislators were wary of delegating power for fear of agency losses in such a broad policy area, legislators also found a positive incentive to be a part of enacting TRA86—a chance to claim credit.

Proposition III. Political Time

A third factor of importance in the question of procedural choice is the notion of political time. There are three broad ways in which this impacted procedural choice. First, as in other cases, a near consensus had emerged such that, in 1986, tax reform constituted "an idea whose time has come." Any law that imposes particularistic costs while delivering general benefits requires at least some semblance of a public willing to endure the costs. Birnbaum and Murray (1987, 285) point out, "the American people were disgusted with the [tax] system, and that disgust represented a latent political force waiting to be tapped." The political weight of such claims can be overdrawn, of course. There is always a certain amount of latent anger on a variety of issues—especially taxes. But congressional action on policy proposals of this sort does not require angry citizens calling their legislators and imploring them to fix a problem. All it needs is that legislators *believe* there is a significant chance citizens *will be* angry on Election Day if Congress does nothing. So despite opinion polls showing that the public was skeptical of tax reform (Conlan, Wrightson, and Beam 1990, 39), Birnbaum and Murray point out,

> Smart politicians knew that beneath the apparent public indifference . . . boiled a potential gusher of discontent that could prove to be a fearsome force. Few members of Congress cherished the thought of ending up on

the wrong side of the popular president's battle against the special interests. They may not have wanted reform, but they were not about to be
seen standing in its way either. (Birnbaum and Murray 1987, 285)

Second, legislators could get behind tax reform because, as we saw above,
the period from 1975 to 1981 had seen the most rapid expansion of tax
expenditures in the nation's history. Ironically, that very expansion helped to
make tax reform a possibility. The previous section argued that one reason
legislators supported tax reform was that the general benefit to be delivered
was sufficiently large that legislators were willing to endure some particularistic pain. Without the expansion of tax expenditures in the 1970s, this incentive would have been lessened.[21]

Finally, the mid-1980s witnessed the rise of an elite consensus on tax
reform. Conlan, Wrightson, and Beam (1990, 240) argue that the enactment
of TRA86 should be attributed, at least in part, to the role played by "policy ideas and professionals, political entrepreneurs, and the news media."
They point out that "by the mid-1980s, most experts—including those within government—were in agreement on basic principles" (1990, 242) of tax
reform. This consensus even extended to members of Congress, some of
whom, the authors claim, "devoutly believed that tax reform should be
enacted because it was 'right' and courageously chose to subordinate their
own electoral interests to this pursuit" (1990, 244–45). That such a consensus among elites existed is incontestable, and there is also little doubt that
many members of Congress shared that view. But precisely because many
members of Congress were true believers in tax reform, very few *were*
required to subordinate their electoral interests to what they believed to be
"right." After all, that very consensus allowed legislative leaders to employ
the procedural tactics with which this study is concerned.

In addition to the general consensus that had emerged to support tax
reform, legislative leaders displayed the requisite sensitivity to the electoral
calendar. There is some evidence to indicate that the political dynamics
unique to divided government were critical to the enactment of TRA86. We
have seen that both Democrats and Republicans were wary of being caught
holding the knife that killed tax reform. But Rostenkowski was also clear in
asserting to Ways and Means Democrats that divided government offered an
opportunity that unified government could not. One member of Congress
who participated in meetings on tax reform with Rostenkowski recalled,

Most of us had made speeches in favor of tax reform at every civic club.
Rostenkowski seized on this and said: "Now you people have been talk-

ing about reforming the tax code and making it fairer for the lower income people, the average working person. You will never get a better opportunity to get this than now because I've got the president on board and he's going to be the lead person out there, which gives everyone cover. If you want to get reform you've got to do it under these circumstances. You can't get it when a Democratic president is out there because you will get slaughtered by the Republicans. But we can get it this year."[22]

In Rostenkowski's view, then, the mid-1980s served as a rare opportunity for tax reform because neither political party could be held solely accountable by the myriad of groups likely to lose favored tax preferences.[23]

It is also important to point out that, just as in the previously examined cases, legislative leaders in TRA86 were very careful to pay attention to the timing of costs and benefits that would be felt by constituents. We have seen that revenue neutrality, distributional neutrality across income classes, and geographic neutrality were key components of tax reform. But legislative leaders were equally careful to ensure that citizens were given tax relief at least at the same time if not before their prized tax preferences would expire. One component common to the House bill, the Senate bill, and the Treasury bill was a so-called stagger. To get to revenue neutrality, each bill had delayed the effective date of the rate reduction by half a year to July 1, 1987. But this would mean rates would go down six months after the elimination of scores of tax preferences. The effective policy result would be that in April 1988, in the middle of the presidential and congressional primary season, millions of middle-income taxpayers would come to the unpleasant realization that tax reform had increased their tax bill by about $700. Eliminating the stagger would cost about $29 billion over five years. While Senate conferees, potential presidential candidates Dole and Bradley aside, were willing to live with the problem, House conferees, all of whom were facing reelection bids, could not. The stagger remained, but the top tax rate was increased from 27 percent to 28 percent. This maneuver moderated the effects of the stagger, particularly on middle- and lower-income taxpayers (Birnbaum and Murray 1987, 270–71). As in other cases, the electoral calendar had constrained the policy possibilities available to legislative leaders.

Finally, and most importantly, TRA86 benefited from the institutional innovation that immediately preceded its enactment. Gary Mucciaroni points out that because of the massive projected budget deficits in the wake of the enactment of the 1981 budget, Congress and the White House had both recognized the need for centralization in decision making on tax policy. This meant that, by 1985, "the atmosphere surrounding Ways and Means had become more conducive to a return to the kind of stronger, more directive leadership that characterized the pre-reform era" (Mucciaroni 1995, 47.) Specifically, there are at least three ways that the Committee had become better equipped to handle tax reform by 1985. First, Arnold (1990, 21) points out that, in seeking to find electorally acceptable ways to raise taxes to combat deficits in the early 1980s, Ways and Means had developed an array of procedural tactics that were familiar and comfortable by 1985. This included drafting bills behind closed doors and the avoidance of roll-call votes. Second, despite efforts to open up Ways and Means bills on the House floor to amendments between 1973 and 1975, the Committee had become more and more successful since then in securing some kind of modified closed rule for consideration on the floor. By 1985, the use of such a rule was no longer groundbreaking (Strahan 1990, 145–46). Finally, the early 1980s also saw a return to the practice of appointing members to the Ways and Means Committee who were considered to be electorally secure. In 1990, Randall Strahan pointed out that,

> Since 1981 neither party has appointed a member who won less than 60 percent of the vote in the previous election. As a result, only four of the thirty-six committee members serving at the time of the tax reform markup in 1985 had won reelection in 1984 by less than a 60 percent margin. In addition, the routine appointment of freshmen members (a practice limited to the Democratic side during the reform era) had also stopped. (Strahan 1990, 146)

Thus, with closed committee hearings, the use of voice votes in committee, the establishment of modified closed rules, and the recruitment of more electorally secure members for Ways and Means, the Committee found itself, by 1985, more capable of handling tax reform than a decade earlier.

All these factors relating to the moment in political time served to influence the question of procedural choice. Legislators chose to handle tax reform on their own because a consensus had emerged in support of reform, because legislators were able to alter the timing of policy effects, and because congressional institutions had developed enhanced capacity to shepherd tax reform to enactment. In short, the moment in political time was right for an internal procedural vehicle.

Proposition IV. Existence of Powerful Champions

Another factor impacting procedural choice in the case of tax reform was the existence of a set of powerful leaders willing to champion the issue. All the procedural tactics employed, all the legislative arm-twisting that went on, and all the media attention that kept rank-and-file legislators focused on the general benefits of tax reform were the result of the efforts of powerful individuals, including President Reagan, Speaker O'Neill, and, of course, the chairmen of the Ways and Means and Finance Committees, Rostenkowski and Packwood. Conlan, Wrightson, and Beam (1990, 221–22) argue that TRA86 succeeded "because a few dogged and well-placed individuals made heroic, if not always purely motivated attempts to save it and because their efforts were grudgingly approved by the optionless majority." Senator Bradley had been out in front pushing the issue of tax reform from the early 1980s until its enactment. And President Reagan had made tax reform a centerpiece of his 1984 State of the Union address and his reelection campaign. But the enactment of TRA86 required more than a public relations strategy. Tax reform could never have succeeded without the "well-placed" individuals who guided the legislative vehicle up, over, and around roadblocks. In arguing that the issue and institutional contexts were critical in enacting tax reform, Gary Mucciaroni also reserves credit for the importance of leadership commitment:

> Those leaders pushed and persuaded reluctant majorities in Congress to address the issue and to approve reform measures. They possessed greater incentives and capacities than nonleaders to champion diffuse interests over specific interests, and their support was an indispensable ingredient for the success of reform efforts. (Mucciaroni 1995, 49)

Such leadership is especially crucial in overcoming the dynamic that led legislators to delegate in the case of base closure. Who will champion the general interest over the particular tax preference defended by a particular fellow member of Congress? In answering this question, several authors point to the critical role played by Chairman Rostenkowski.

Rostenkowski's fervor for tax reform was exceeded by many, including Bradley. But Rostenkowski offered two things that Bradley could not. First, Rostenkowski's key institutional position as Chairman of Ways and Means meant that only he could get the ball rolling on TRA86. His institutional advantages allowed him to employ the full array of procedural tactics in support of tax reform, including closing committee hearings, handing out transition rules to key legislators inside and outside the committee, and monopolizing control of staff expertise. The frequent use of this last tactic led one member of the Ways and Means Committee to remark, "if I had really wanted to influence the way the actual law was written, I would have applied for a job on the Joint Tax or Ways and Means staff."[24]

A second characteristic that Rostenkowski's leadership offered that Bradley's could not was his particular style. Birnbaum and Murray describe it best:

> The effort needed a strong hand to guide it, and that was what Rostenkowski provided. At times, he bullied his members; at other times, he cajoled and begged them. When necessary, as with the state and local deduction, he simply bought their support. It was the kind of one-on-one wheeling and dealing that the Chicago pol knew best. Rostenkowski's methods were rooted in something that transcended traditional explanations of legislative success, such as seniority or leadership position or political quid pro quos. The methods were wrapped up in the man himself. (Birnbaum and Murray 1987, 132)

Characteristics such as these led Conlan, Wrightson, and Beam (1990, 84) to refer to Rostenkowski as "the single most important factor contributing to congressional passage of the Tax Reform Act of 1986."

There is a sense, then, in which the unpredictable force of personality played a significant role in enacting TRA86. It is beyond the scope of this study to speculate on why Rostenkowski, or Packwood, Reagan, O'Neill, or Bradley for that matter, wanted to take on tax reform. Others have done so in their accounts of the saga. The relevant point for our purposes is that TRA86 did attract powerful champions inside the normal legislative process and that impacted the question of procedural choice.

Proposition V. The One, the Few, and the Many

The fifth proposition suggests that the larger the number of groups that have to suffer the particularistic pain, the more likely the Congress is to employ an extra-congressional procedure. At first glance, the procedures employed in dealing with TRA86 would seem to refute this proposition. After all, as we saw in Table 5.2, *many* tax expenditure provisions were repealed, limited, or modified in ways that served up particularistic pain for a wide variety of groups. Indeed, the vast number of groups that paid the price for the rate relief in TRA86 is the main reason so many marvel that the idea was ever enacted into law. So why did members of Congress choose to deliver all this particularistic pain personally when they could have handed the unpleasant task off to some other person, or institution, or formula?

A first answer to this question was discussed earlier. Legislative leaders quickly realized that enacting TRA86 offered credit-claiming opportunities that narrower policy areas could not. Because the scope of the policy area was so broad, the general benefit came to have real meaning for legislative leaders and the rank and file alike. In short, this fifth proposition was turned on its head. We might say that the policy had reached a tipping point where so many groups were sacrificing that the delivery of the general benefit was sufficiently large for members of Congress to *want* to enact TRA86 on their own.

A second answer would be a cautionary note having to do with the nature of the theory advanced in this book and the propositions that comprise it. Each individual proposition presented here is not an ironclad rule but rather an expressed tendency or likelihood. Each is one of several factors in determining procedural choice. So we need not accept that a violation of one proposition in one case invalidates the theory or even that it disproves that individual proposition. We can see that in the case of TRA86, the vast majority of the evidence supports the overall theory advanced here. And, as we have seen in the several cases presented in this book, each of these propositions is a necessary part of any comprehensive theory of procedural choice.

Conclusion

In this chapter, we have seen a variety of reasons why legislators chose to handle tax reform internally rather than rely on some sort of extra-congressional procedure. Handling the bill internally allowed legislators to protect more politically sensitive geographically concentrated tax benefits. Handling the bill internally allowed legislators not only to avoid the prohibitive agency losses that attend delegating power in such a broad policy area, but also to claim credit for the larger general benefit that attends such broad policy areas. Legislators found themselves at a moment in political time when the institutional capacity of Congress was well-suited to handling tax reform internally. Finally, powerful champions of tax reform emerged from within the normal legislative process that had both the institutional position and the legislative skills necessary to shepherd TRA86 past legislative hurdles.

One final point about tax reform, touched upon earlier, merits discussion. In assessing the lessons to be learned from the story of tax reform, Randall Strahan argues,

> The politics and the outcome in the tax reform case directly contradict the basic assumptions about committee behavior derived from the electoral connection model. Both the prominence of appeals to members' concerns with good public policy in Chairman Dan Rostenkowski's coalition-building strategy, and an outcome in which broad, diffuse, and poorly organized interests were advanced over those of well-organized clientele groups show that congressional politics, in at least some cases, are more complex

than Mayhew's [1974] model assumes. To put it simply, a theoretical framework that incorporates goals other than reelection is needed to explain the politics and outcome in this case. (Strahan 1990, 157)

Similarly, we saw earlier that because of the high degree of elite consensus on the need for tax reform, Conlan, Wrightson, and Beam (1990, 245) argue that some members of Congress "courageously chose to subordinate their own electoral interests to this pursuit."

That members of Congress have goals other than reelection is no doubt true. But while they may not be single-minded, it is equally non-controversial to assert that even the most policy-oriented members of Congress "care intensely about reelection."[25] Fortunately for them, however, if this account of tax reform teaches us anything, it is that the choice Conlan, Wrightson, and Beam suggest is a false one. Policy-oriented legislators are just as adept and likely to utilize procedural tactics that reshape the calculus of legislative decision making, creating an environment where their policy interests *do not contradict* electoral interests. In his assessment of the politics of tax reform, Douglas Arnold makes the point more eloquently:

> These procedural strategies *allowed* legislators to reform the tax system, but they did not *force* legislators to do so. At each stage legislators had to agree to tie their own hands, and most of their decisions to limit the range of choice were unaffected by electoral calculations. When legislators decided to meet in secrecy, to delegate difficult decisions to the chairmen, to prohibit amendments, or to require that amendments be revenue neutral, they were declaring that they were personally in favor of tax reform. If legislators had been personally opposed to tax reform, all they had to do was insist that the sun must shine on any tax bill, knowing that sunshine would have destroyed tax reform. It is hardly surprising that many legislators were disgusted with the current tax system, but it is a healthy reminder about the limits of electoral explanations to recall that legislators' own personal policy preferences were necessary conditions for tax reform. (Arnold 1990, 222–23, original emphasis)

Thus, it is not contradictory to suggest that legislators have policy preferences that transcend electoral politics while also suggesting that legislators constantly pay attention to the electoral implications of their actions. Because legislators are able to shape the context within which they make decisions, they are able to have it both ways. They can do the right thing *and* protect their electoral interests at the same time.

SIX

Conclusion

The cases examined in the preceding chapters are worthy of our attention in the budgetary climate of 2005. An era of structural budget deficits appears to have returned and it likely will not be long before we see legislative leaders searching for ways to make particularistic cuts in favor of the general benefit of deficit reduction. These cases thus provide some comfort to those who believe Congress is incapable or permanently unwilling to make these sorts of hard choices. Legislative leaders do, in fact, sometimes seek to enact policies like these and those leaders who are successful in enacting these policies are not alone in this struggle. They do not impose procedural strategies on an unwilling constituency. Rank-and-file legislators are active co-conspirators in these undertakings because legislative institutions, as we have seen, are routinely a matter of majoritarian choice.

When and why legislative leaders and the rank-and-file legislators who support them choose to "do the right thing" are, for the most part, questions outside the scope of this study.[1] Here, we have been more interested in examining *how* legislators enact such policies and why they choose the particular procedural paths they do. In the opening chapter, a theory of procedural choice was developed and, in subsequent chapters, that theory was applied to four different cases. In this chapter, we will examine how well that theory held up when tested by those cases and make some suggestions about future avenues of research. We will also quickly revisit each of the policy areas in question and expand on the contemporary relevance of these stories. But first, it is useful to make a couple of observations about delegation, procedural manipulation, and democratic accountability.

Procedures, Democracy, and the Public Interest

Beauty Is in the Eye of the Beholder

The manipulation of procedures by legislative leaders is frequently portrayed as a normative evil. We are led to imagine the proverbial "smoke-filled room" in which elite party bosses make decisions for the benefit of the few at the expense of the many. Along the same lines, many view the use of the types of legislative procedures described in this book as irresponsible, evasive,[2] and out of line with our collective sense of democratic accountability.

That elites and well-organized interests sometimes benefit disproportionately from an insider game is no doubt true. But the cases discussed here suggest that sometimes procedures are manipulated to benefit the many at the expense of the few. Indeed, the argument has been advanced here that, at times, only through closed-door meetings, omnibus legislative vehicles, and delegation to unelected officials can the public interest be advanced over the narrow interest. Similarly, the notion that legislators are incapable of being responsible and accountable to the electorate because of the use of these procedures would seem to confuse the means and the ends of democracy. In most of these cases, legislators are freeing themselves to be more accountable to certain types of interests—general interests—that are not as well organized and that do not participate in the political process in the same ways. So long as those interests are being represented some of the time, it is fair to conclude that legislators are being responsible and accountable. Indeed, they are behaving as we should hope our elected representatives would.

In this light, we are drawn to the conclusion that while there may be "good" policies and "bad" policies, there are no "bad" procedures. The procedures themselves are morally neutral and can be put to use for the general interest or for parochial interests. It is my hope that this book has helped to foster a greater appreciation of the importance of procedural mechanisms, whether they are part of the more routine legislative process or extra-congressional. The deft manipulation of procedures can absolutely change policy outcomes for the worse or the better. Thus, procedural beauty is truly in the eye of the beholder.

There's Delegation and Then There's Delegation

This study has also yielded useful insights on the nature of congressional delegation. Some view congressional delegation of authority negatively,[3] and others have a more sympathetic view of it, but most scholars assume a far more bipolar understanding of delegation than is appropriate. The general impression seems to be that power is thrown over a wall and is exercised without congressional influence or interference. That, for instance, is the widespread view of how Congress dealt with the problems of base closure and NAFTA. While Congress did delegate authority in these cases, I have found that the procedures employed are far less *extra*-congressional than most of the literature assumes.

The standard interpretation of trade policy in general, and NAFTA in particular, is that legislators are confronted with a collective-action problem in which individually rational behavior—in this case particularistic protectionism—is collectively irrational, and so legislators delegate policymaking authority to an agent—the president—who is understood to be institutionally immune to the collective-action problem. But, as we saw, legislators delegated far less authority to the president than is commonly understood and only delegated what authority they did because of the foreign policy nature of the policy problem. Similarly, in the case of base closure, where legislators clearly delegated a relatively greater amount of authority, that delegation was tempered in significant ways that are not commonly recognized or understood. For instance, legislators imposed requirements in the first round of closures that ruled out for consideration foreign bases and required that any closure would have to be shown to recover its costs within six years, effectively ruling out large bases whose cleanup and relocation costs would be too high to recover quickly.

So while Congress does frequently delegate authority, appearances can be deceiving. Before scholars ask why legislators would ever voluntarily tie their own hands, they need to look a bit closer at the knot. It isn't black and white and the knot usually isn't as tight as we think. Here again, we are likely to notice a scholarly choir singing an overly negative hymn. When Congress delegates, scholars accuse legislators of abdicating their responsibility. When Congress *appears* to delegate, but retains significant influence over policy outcomes, scholars accuse legislators of meddling. Legislators can't seem to win—at least not when scholars are the judges.

A Theory of Procedural Choice

It is now useful to turn our attention back to the place where we started. Why do legislators use the procedures they do? Why do they sometimes delegate to varying degrees in overcoming collective-action problems, and why do they sometimes use the internal institutions and procedures of the Congress to accomplish similar ends? While a quantifiable answer is elusive, the five propositions examined in this study have each proven to be important determinants of procedural choice.

1. Geographic Concentration of Costs

In the four case studies, we have seen empirical support for an important point implied by Douglas Arnold. Arnold (1990, 26) argues that the distinction between particularistic costs and benefits that are geographically concentrated and those that are not is useful because geographically concentrated groups that receive the benefits or pay the costs are, by definition, more directly represented in Congress and have an easier time overcoming organizational barriers. In each case we found many examples where legislators did indeed display greater sensitivity to geographically concentrated costs. And, importantly, we found that this enhanced sensitivity played an important role in procedural choice. Legislators, for instance, chose to delegate authority to draw up a list of military bases to be closed because the costs of the policy were so geographically concentrated as to make it politically unfeasible to handle the matter within Congress. In choosing a single high-level nuclear waste site for the nation, the Congress struggled for more than ten years to find an internal procedural path to gang up on Nevada's small and weak congressional delegation. In designing procedures to enact a free-trade agreement with Mexico and Canada, legislators delegated some authority, but were sure to leave themselves leverage at a variety of points in the process so that they would be able to protect the most sensitive trade benefits—those that are geographically concentrated—in their states and districts. Finally, and perhaps most tellingly, in the case of tax reform, legislators settled on an internal procedure that would leave to legislators the tough choices about which tax expenditures would be spared and which eliminated. Again, it was the geographically concentrated tax expenditures that were advantaged.

The particular sensitivity of geographically concentrated costs thus has two implications for students of collective-action problems in Congress. First, in the search for cuts in particularistic benefits or expansion of particularistic costs, geographically concentrated benefits and costs do have a privileged position. Second, when legislators do decide to impose geographically concentrated costs, they are likely to delegate authority to impose those costs.

2. Scope of the Policy Area

A distinction has been advanced between "broad" and "narrow" policy areas. Despite the lack of a quantifiable index of their scope,, it is clear from the evidence presented here that the relative broadness or narrowness of a policy area is an important determinant in procedural choice. All other things being equal, legislators are more likely to delegate authority in a narrow policy area and less likely to do so in a broad policy area because of the difference in the ability of legislators to contain agency losses[4] in the two different types of areas. Because military installations policy is a relatively narrow policy area both in terms of its fiscal impact and its relative lack of impact on other policy areas, legislators found delegation an attractive procedural alternative. On the other hand, because reforming the tax code impacted virtually every policy area and had the potential to touch virtually every penny the federal government collects, legislators never even seriously considered delegating authority in enacting TRA86. Similarly, in the case of NAFTA, legislators delegated only to the extent necessary to carry on international negotiations. Finally, the relatively small amount of power delegated in the case of nuclear waste disposal was delegated only after legislators had found ways to narrow the scope of the agent's discretion.

Narrow policy areas do not require delegation. It is more accurate to say that the ability of legislators to contain agency losses is a precondition of delegation. The more narrow a policy area, the easier it is to contain those losses because there is less room for agents to whom power has been delegated to make policy in conflict with legislators' preferences.

3. Political Time

It is equally clear from the cases examined in this study that the moment in political time impacts the question of procedural choice in three important ways. First, while some measure of consensus is required for legislative leaders to seek to resolve these collective-action problems in the first place, the greater that consensus, the easier it is for legislators to pursue an internal procedural strategy. Second, institutional evolution plays an important role. Procedural choice is very much a function of the particular institutional avenues that are available and politically feasible. When a history of mistrust has developed between Congress and an agent, delegation may be proscribed. When institutions necessary to impose costs on particularistic groups are lacking within the Congress, an internal procedural pathway is likewise proscribed. Third, legislative leaders must time policy decisions and effects so as to maximize electoral benefits and minimize electoral costs. Sometimes, delegating authority may offer the best route to delaying the imposition of those costs.

Each of these cases displayed sensitivity to most, if not all, of these points. In base closure, for instance, the perception among legislators of a history of abuse of the base closure process by presidents and the Pentagon constrained the choices of agents to whom power could be delegated. One cannot understand why legislators chose to create an independent commission in the case of base closure without understanding that historical development. Similarly, the Ways and Means Committee was able to draft a significant revenue-neutral tax reform bill in 1986 because of institutional developments in the years prior to tax reform that strengthened the committee's ability to resist the particularistic demands of "Gucci Gulch." Senator Paul Laxalt's (R-NV) departure from the Senate cleared the way for Congress to choose Yucca Mountain as the nation's sole high-level nuclear waste repository. It is quite possible Nevada's delegation would have been able to hold out longer with the aid of the president's closest friend in the Senate. Finally, reverse fast-track procedures, added because of legislators' displeasure with President Reagan's handling of the U.S.–Canada Free Trade Agreement, were an important insurance factor in a close vote for legislators deciding whether to reauthorize fast-track authority during the negotiation of NAFTA. The moment in political time thus captures an important element of procedural choice. Legislators are constrained by elite and public opinion, by institutional developments that precede their actions, and by the electoral calendar.

4. Existence of Powerful Champions

Another important factor is the existence of legislative leaders who are willing to champion the cause of particularistic cuts in favor of general benefits. It isn't hard to imagine that, in any reasonable model of legislative behavior, the legislator who seeks to impose costs on particular, identifiable, well-organized groups in favor of a general benefit for which few will be able to credibly claim credit is unlikely to be popular. Yet the existence of such a character is an important precondition in the pursuit of an internal procedural strategy. Base closure attracted no such person and extensive delegation was the procedural answer. In a relatively close vote on both the House and Senate floors on NAFTA, it mattered that key party leaders were supporters. More importantly, President Clinton pursued a full-court press strategy in rounding up votes. Tax reform attracted *all* the key legislative leaders, including Speaker O'Neill, Chairman Rostenkowski, Chairman Packwood, and President Reagan. One reason for this was that the general benefit was so large that there was credit to be claimed for being connected with the popular legislation. Nuclear waste disposal attracted powerful legislative leaders, including Chairman Johnston, Speaker Wright, and Majority Leader Foley, who were each attempting to stick the waste in Nevada to keep it out of their own states. Regardless of motivation, however, the important point here is not why powerful legislative leaders championed these causes but simply that they did. With these well-positioned champions, internal procedural manipulation became a realistic possibility.

5. The One, the Few, and the Many

The last important factor examined in this study that impacts procedural choice is simply the quantity of particularistic groups that are impacted. The case of nuclear waste disposal differed from base closure in that only one location was to bear the burden of particularistic costs. Containing costs to one location makes it easier for legislators to avoid delegation both because of the legislative math involved—fewer legislators objecting and a greater number of legislators are supportive as they are off the hook—and because it becomes easier to compensate a smaller number of groups. For this reason, legislators were able to determine a site for a national nuclear waste repository on their own.

Putting It All Together

Putting these five propositions together, a generalizable theory of procedural choice emerges. The theory that emerges is to be considered as a whole rather than as the sum of its parts. As we have seen, no single proposition is determinative in itself and, in places, a proposition or two may even be violated. Yet taken as a whole, the theory can be considered predictive. Each of the individual propositions has shown itself to be a recurring and important factor in procedural choice across a diverse set of cases. As a new era of structural deficits appears to be emerging, it is clear that opportunities to further test the theory will not be hard to find.

In searching for new places to test this theory, members of Congress will likely oblige scholars by reverting to the very same policy problems that inspire the cases in this book. For instance, despite the significant amount of mistrust and anger that developed as a result of the last round of base closures in 1995, Congress has scheduled a new round of closures for 2005.[5] Similarly, in 2002, Congress enacted legislation granting the president fast-track negotiating authority for the first time since NAFTA was enacted ten years earlier.[6] Meanwhile, even though opponents of the Yucca Mountain Project have been able to delay, though not derail, construction of the nuclear waste repository, the amount of commercial nuclear waste piling up will soon require that Congress find a second site—or a second solution—to the same problem. Finally, just as the Reagan tax cuts of 1981 served as the precursor to TRA86 by creating a sense of unfairness in the tax code, the Bush tax cuts twenty years later have the potential to spur new calls for tax fairness and tax reform.

In addition to revisiting the very same issues discussed in this book, the Congress will likely be facing other similar kinds of policy problems. To mention two, record surpluses have been replaced by record deficits and Medicare and Social Security are likely to flirt with crisis in the near future.

Each of these policy areas is one that will require legislators to find ways to impose particularistic costs in favor of diffuse, general benefits. This study has offered a glimpse of how legislative leaders have confronted and managed these kinds of policy problems in a variety of inventive ways and has offered an explanation about how procedural choices were made. A next logical step for scholars is to continue to apply and test the theory advanced here across a larger number of cases using a wider variety of empirical techniques. It is not every day that history repeats itself so that political scientists can refine and enhance their theories. While that is probably not the motivating impulse behind these policy problems, clearly political scientists should take advantage of the opportunity to study a Congress struggling to "do the right thing" in a host of areas over the coming decade.

How to Do the Right Thing? It Depends

Speaking more generally of strategies utilized by coalition leaders to overcome legislative roadblocks, Douglas Arnold (1990, 91) argues, "there are no universal strategies, appropriate for any proposal under any conditions. Leaders must tailor general strategies to fit the idiosyncrasies of specific policy proposals." This study builds on Arnold's important work by attempting to sketch out some general tendencies leaders exhibit in tailoring procedural strategies in imposing particularistic costs in favor of general benefits. Arnold constructs a workable theory of legislative behavior meant to explain the total universe of policy outcomes. His prescription to legislative leaders attempting to "do the right thing" but unsure of the procedural path to take must necessarily be, "it depends." At the very least, the theory of procedural choice advanced here helps us to explain what it depends upon. Legislators can close military bases, close special interest tax loopholes, designate a national site for nuclear waste, and overcome their particularistic proclivities in trade policy *under the right conditions*. We have seen that those *right conditions* are diverse, explainable, and within the realm of legislative leaders' control.

Because those conditions are influenced by legislative leaders and because these types of policy problems are becoming more common, Barbara Sinclair has correctly pointed out that our textbook understanding of how a bill becomes a law no longer describes the contemporary legislative process. She (Sinclair 2000, 221) argues, "congressional actors—especially congressional majority party leaders but also individual senators and the Senate minority party—now have more choices, and the alternatives they choose lead to different legislative processes." The findings here build upon Sinclair's conclusion in two ways. First, the remarkable diversity of procedures utilized in these cases corroborates Sinclair's finding that the choices available to legislative leaders is seemingly limited only by their own imagination and political acumen. That is not a very significant limit at all. Specifically, the rich detail of these cases argues for applying Sinclair's findings to the even *more* unorthodox legislative procedures—extra-congressional ones. These are, after all, *legislative* procedures and deserve more of our attention. Second, expanding on this latter point, it is my hope that this study has contributed in some way to a better understanding of those "different legislative processes." The procedural choices legislative leaders make are not random and they do have important implications for governmental accountability and democracy.

Doing the right thing, as it has been defined in this book, is not easy, and it is rarely elegant or pretty by the standard of the textbook legislative process. But it is far more common than much of the literature leads us to believe. A better understanding of the factors that allow legislators to do the right thing should lead scholars and their students alike to see the inner beauty of these procedural beasts.

NOTES

Notes to Chapter One

1. I draw my use of this phrase, in part, from Jacobson (2001, 223). Jacobson briefly discusses base closure and other cases like it in a section of chapter 7 of his book called "Doing the Right Thing."

2. I have borrowed the descriptions "general, late-order" and "particularistic, early-order" from Arnold (1990). The terms are meant to suggest continua on which various benefits and costs may be placed. General benefits are those shared equally by all citizens and they are juxtaposed with particularistic benefits that are shared by certain people based on their inclusion in some fixed group delineated by age, sex, race, ethnicity, hobby, occupation, and so on. Early-order benefits and costs are those that are more quickly and visibly the result of some action taken by government. Thus, the particular policies being discussed are those that impose costs on a concentrated group in the short term in order to realize some benefit for a more broad and diffuse public later on.

3. Some evidence of the "newness" of these procedures is suggested by changes in the various editions of Gary C. Jacobson's *The Politics of Congressional Elections* (2001). In a chapter on the relationship between congressional elections and the internal politics of Congress, Jacobson argues that the pursuit of reelection does not necessarily translate into the ability to legislate in the national interest. The politics of Congress, he suggests, is characterized by a host of diseases which Jacobson discusses in different sections. Among these sections are "Particularism," "Serving the Organized," "Immobility," and "Symbolism." In the third, fourth, and fifth editions, published in 1993, 1997, and 2001 respectively, Jacobson adds a new section called "Doing the Right Thing," in which he points out that sometimes Congress does legislate in favor of the public interest at the expense of particular interests. Importantly for our purposes, he uses the fast-track process and the base-closure commission as his examples of "doing the right thing." In a puzzling passage, Jacobson (2001, 192) argues, "instances of this sort are the exception rather than the rule, but they are by no means rare."

4. It is true that very often, in the authorization of an agency, the legislative language in a law contains a so-called sunset provision that technically makes them ad hoc institutions as well. There still remains a difference between these cases and extra-

congressional procedures, however. Extra-congressional procedures are designed for very specific rounds of policy effects. The base-closure commission existed only to come up with four lists of bases. On the other hand, even agencies that are created with sunset provisions have comparatively wide latitude to carry out their actions up to the date prescribed in the legislation.

5. See, for instance, Hager and Pianin (1996). For an excellent treatment of the role of independent commissions, see Campbell (2002, 50), who lists a variety of subjects for which commissions have been proposed and includes base closure in the same category as proposed commissions on entitlements that have no formal authority to do anything other than study issues and write reports. Nevertheless, Campbell does view the increasing use of commissions as part of a larger pattern he describes as "the use of alternative mechanisms in formulating policy" (131).

6. In this sense, it is actually quite surprising that Congress does not utilize these extra-congressional procedures more often. If Arnold is correct in arguing that legislators are more worried about avoiding blame than with claiming credit, the focus shifts from a question of why members would voluntarily give power and authority away to one of why they don't do it more often.

7. Remarkably little attention has been paid to the use of extra-congressional procedures as a trend. Rourke and Schulman (1989, 131) argue that "no development in modern American politics has been more striking than the habit the country has fallen into of creating a wide variety of instant organizations and charging them with the task of coming up with solutions to the most pressing problems of public policy." Their discussion is focused more broadly, however, on all sorts of temporary bureaucracies, including study commissions and task forces with no formal authority. A variety of other authors note the similarity between many of these mechanisms but do not attempt to develop any model of procedural choice. See, for instance, Deering (1996, 168n20) and Mayer (1995, 411n3).

8. In his seminal piece on Congress, Mayhew (1974, 56–57) recognizes the distinction in his discussion of credit-claiming by pointing out, "a final point here has to do with geography. The examples given so far are all of benefits conferred upon home constituencies or recipients therein. . . . But the properties of particularized benefits were carefully specified so as not to exclude the possibility that some benefits may be given to recipients outside the home constituencies. Some probably are. Narrowly drawn tax loopholes qualify as particularized benefits, and some of them are probably conferred upon recipients outside the home districts. (It is difficult to find solid evidence on this point.) Campaign contributions flow into districts from the outside, so it would not be surprising to find that benefits go where the resources are." In another example, Weingast and Marshall (1988, 136–37) point out, "interest groups are not uniformly distributed. They typically have concentrations of voters in particular locations." The authors go on to argue that members are thus more sensitive to constituencies within their district:

> In the competition for interest group support, specific representatives have a comparative advantage. The lack of complete fungibility of votes implies that legislators are advantaged in attracting support from interest

groups located in their district (see Denzau and Munger 1986). This advantage arises because service to local interests attracts both votes and organized resources for the district's representative. Service to this group by an outsider, in contrast, attracts only the latter and may lose votes.

Finally, in reviewing the work of distributive theorists, Krehbiel (1991, 26) argues, "the key point is that distributive theories consistently presume that legislators' preferences are geographically based and therefore that legislative decision making provides opportunities for *gains from trade*" (original italics).

9. For his part, Arnold (1990, 141) argues, "Competition for geographic benefits has only modest effects on the shape of public policy when programs provide abundant general benefits" and that legislators "seldom support programs simply because they wish to obtain such benefits." But he also goes on to point out, "the policy effects are actually greater on the downside—when geographic benefits are to be curtailed." Indeed, the "downside" is the precise type of case under examination here.

10. These "agency losses" could come in a variety of forms. The agent may have different policy preferences than the principal. Additionally, because the principal in this case is the Congress, a body made up of many principals, the agent may be loyal to or act on behalf of only some of the principals. Finally, the principal also incurs losses in the process of monitoring the agent to be sure the foregoing losses are avoided.

11. "Broad" and "narrow" policy areas are admittedly vague terms in need of clarification. There is no precise index by which to measure the scope of a policy area, but two characteristics of policy areas can help us to classify them in relation to one another. First, by a "broad" policy area, I mean one that cuts across other issue areas in a more substantive way. By a "narrow" policy area, I mean one that impacts a lesser number of other policy areas in a lesser way. It is true, of course, that virtually every piece of legislation could be argued to have an impact on multiple policy areas and it is also true that it is impossible to quantify the level of impact a particular policy area has on another. But it is equally clear that some policy areas impact others in a relatively greater way than others. For instance, fiscal policy clearly impacts a broader number of policy areas than endangered species policy in more substantive kinds of ways. Second, policy areas may be categorized according to their fiscal impact. Though this is a crude measure that offers little insight into the nature of some policy areas that have nothing to do with money, it is clear, on the other hand, that a bill that closes ten military bases is significantly more narrow than an omnibus deficit reduction bill that raises income taxes and cuts spending in a host of programs and entitlements. Clearly, the point in this instance is that military base closure is a more narrow policy area than comprehensive tax reform. Where exactly the line is drawn between "broad" and "narrow" is unimportant for our purposes. All that matters is the recognition that one is more narrow in relation to the other.

12. For instance, Mayer (1995) argues that members of Congress were willing to delegate as much authority as they did in the case of base closures not only because the particular procedure employed limited "the domain of the agent's authority" in a wide variety of ways, but also because the policy area itself was sufficiently narrow that the potential costs of delegation had a natural limit.

13. For more on this concept, see Weaver (1986).

14. Among others, John Kingdon (1995) offers an excellent treatment of how issues move on and off the public agenda. This book, and this proposition, is not particularly concerned with why issues like these make their way onto the agenda, but is interested in the question of how issues do so. Kingdon asks in the title to the opening chapter of his classic book, *How Does an Idea's Time Come?* (1995, 19), to which he answers, "if any one set of participants in the policy process is important in the shaping of the agenda, it is elected officials and their appointees, rather than career bureaucrats or nongovernmental actors." He adds, "a visible cluster made up of such actors as the president and prominent members of Congress" has the greatest effect on the agenda.

15. What motivates legislative leaders is the subject of a vast and time-worn literature. See, for instance, Mayhew (1974) and Fenno (1973).

16. This is not an uncontroversial claim, as my discussion of the Yucca Mountain Project (see chapter 3) will reveal.

17. Representative Dick Armey (R-TX) quoted in *Congressional Record,* October 12, 1988, H30039.

Notes to Chapter Two

1. This concept has become conventional wisdom among political scientists. For instance, see Arnold (1990, 32) and Weaver (1986).

2. PL 100–526, approved October 24, 1988.

3. A joint resolution requires the signature of the president and it is fair to assume the president would be supportive of a list approved by and forwarded to the Congress by the secretary of defense. Effectively, this means that Congress could only stop a list of base closures and realignments by overriding a presidential veto, which requires a $^2/_3$ vote.

4. PL 101–510, approved November 5, 1990.

5. An unidentified staff member of the Armed Services Committee quoted in Dexter (1969, 182).

6. The override vehicle was PL 105–159 overriding President Clinton's rescissions from PL 105–45 (the FY 1998 military construction appropriations bill).

7. Hadwiger (1993, 51). These figures appear to be a matter of some controversy. Twight (1990, 241–42) reports the figures as 73 bases (37 in the U.S.) in March 1961, 33 bases in December 1963, 63 bases in April 1964, 95 bases in November 1964, and 149 bases in December 1965. For our purposes, the exact figures are not relevant. It is sufficient to say that the Department of Defense was regularly releasing lists of significant numbers of base closures.

8. Speaking in general of the changes in Congress during the late 1960s and early 1970s, Shepsle (1989, 264) argues, "the slow accretion of resources permitted members to respond to the changes in their home districts and encouraged them to cross the boundaries of specialization. These developments began to erode the reciprocity, deference, and division of labor that defined the textbook Congress."

9. For greater detail on this line of argument, see Twight (1990, 255–62).

10. Senator Carl Levin (D-MI) quoted in *Congressional Record,* May 10, 1988, S10197.

11. In addition to the many scholars I have cited in favor of this general proposition, it is important to note that many others cite base closure as the prime example of how geographic benefits are more sensitive than non-geographic benefits. See, for instance, Lindsay (1990). Significantly, Lindsay finds that parochial concerns intrude on defense policy decisions far less than the political science literature would suggest, but that military installations policy is the most notable exception to this rule.

12. For a more detailed defense of this argument, see Arnold (1990, 26).

13. Senator Phil Gramm (R-TX) quoted in Dick Armey (1988, 74).

14. Representative John Kasich (R-OH) quoted in *Congressional Record,* July 7, 1988, H17079.

15. I draw this concept from Arnold (1990, 47–51).

16. Armey (1988, 73).

17. Senator Alan Dixon (D-IL) quoted in *Congressional Record,* May 9, 1988, S10142.

18. Representative Frank Horton (R-NY) quoted in *Congressional Record,* July 7, 1988, H17063.

19. Senator Carl Levin (D-MI) quoted in *Congressional Record,* May 10, 1988, S10197.

20. See the remarks of Senator William Cohen (R-ME) in *Congressional Record,* May 10, 1988, S10223.

21. Representative Jim Kolbe (R-AZ) quoted in *Congressional Record,* July 7, 1988, H17065.

22. Representative Dick Armey (R-TX) quoted in *Congressional Record,* July 7, 1988, H17072.

23. Representative John Porter (R-IL) quoted in *Congressional Record,* July 12, 1988, H17743.

24. The amendment was defeated, but restrictions of this sort did eventually find their way into the final version of the bill. Defense Secretary Frank Carlucci had created the commission without congressional approval earlier in the year and the plan was that the commission was to report to the Secretary by the end of the year. The Armey bill was seeking to provide legal sanction for the Secretary of Defense to implement the commission's recommendations. It would therefore be difficult to terminate all of the existing commission staff and hire entirely new staff so late in the process. Porter and Senator Dixon were partially successful, however, in arranging for a compromise. The final 1988 bill did impose controls on the portion of commission staff directly from the Pentagon and expand the number of commissioners, and congressional leaders were informally a part of the process of selecting the new members of the commission. See, for instance, the remarks of Senator Sam Nunn (D-GA) quoted in *Congressional Record,* October 12, 1988, S29888.

25. Representative Jon Kyl (R-AZ) quoted in *Congressional Record,* July 12, 1988, H17751.

26. Representative Dick Armey (R-TX) quoted in *Congressional Record,* July 12, 1988, H17753.

27. Representative William Dickinson (R-AL) quoted in *Congressional Record,* July 7, 1988, H17057.

28. Representative William Dickinson (R-AL) quoted in *Congressional Record,* July 12, 1988, H17745.

29. Representative Joel Hefley (R-CO) quoted in *Congressional Record,* July 12, 1988, H17776.

30. These two factors also came together in 1908, 1920, 1928, 1960, 1968, and 2000.

31. Representative Les Aspin (D-WI) quoted in *Congressional Record,* July 12, 1988, H17747.

32. Representative William Dickinson (R-AL) quoted in *Congressional Record,* July 12, 1988, H17747.

33. Morrison (1989, 801) reports that House Armed Services Committee Chairman, Les Aspin, estimated "a hundred or more congressmen are worried that bases in their districts might be closed." But Aspin went on to point out that most of those "will breathe a sigh of relief" once the base list comes out. Some members probably had more reason for concern than others as bases in their districts had been on prior DOD closure lists. But the number of members falling into this category was limited.

34. Benenson (1990, 87).

35   Vick (1995, A21).

36. See for instance, Hadwiger (1993, 218–39) and Cook (1993).

37. Mills (1988, 3629).

38. Mills (1989, 662).

39. Ibid.

40. See for instance, Hadwiger (1993, 195–217). Describing such efforts in the wake of the 1988 closure list, Hadwiger points out that a few efforts to keep open some facilities on or near bases being closed were successful. Similarly, President Clinton, along with the California and Texas delegations, worked to privatize a number of jobs lost as a result of the closure of Air Force depots in those states. While this effort was successful, it so alienated members of the delegations from states where these privatized jobs were supposed to go, that it was the key reason another round of base closures was not approved during Clinton's presidency. See for instance, Dewar (1997).

41. Senator Alan Dixon (D-IL) quoted in Palmer (1994).

42. Ibid.

43. William Cohen quoted in Kitfield (1997).

44. Representative Dick Armey (R-TX) quoted in Dewar (1997).

45. This view echoes the view of delegation generally asserted by Kiewiet and McCubbins (1991, 3). They challenge the predominant view of political scientists that Congress abdicates its responsibilities for crafting difficult policy solutions because it lacks strong centralized leadership. They argue, "the alternative we pose to the abdication hypothesis is that it is possible to delegate authority to others and yet continue to achieve desired outcomes. Indeed, it is often the case that desired outcomes can be achieved *only* by delegating authority to others."

Notes to Chapter Three

1. Some may argue that the Yucca Mountain Project can hardly be described as an example of Congress "doing the right thing." I address this point later in this chapter.

2. Updated statistics can be found online at [www.nei.org]. Also see Gross (1998, 134).

3. Also see Carter (1987, 145–46).

4. Later on, this prevision was changed to bring the nuclear waste trust fund back 'on-budget' to mask the size of the federal budget.

5. The measure passed by a voice vote in the Senate and by a 256–32 margin in the House.

6. Senator Larry Craig (R-ID) quoted in Idelson (1991a, 2558).

7. Governor Kenny Guinn (R-NV) did officially veto the Yucca Mountain Project on April 8, 2002. His veto was overridden by both houses of Congress later that summer and, as a result, Nevada will be taking the nation's nuclear waste without *any* compensation.

8. Senator J. Bennett Johnston (D-LA) quoted in *Congressional Record,* December 21, 1987, 37693.

9. Sen. Johnston quoted in *Congressional Record,* December 21, 1987, 37694.

10. Representative Morris Udall (D-AZ) quoted in *Congressional Record,* December 21, 1987, 37068.

11. Rep. Udall quoted in *Congressional Record,* December 21, 1988, 37069.

12. Representative Philip Sharp (D-IN) quoted in *Congressional Record,* December 21, 1987, 37069.

13. Representative Douglas Owens (D-UT) quoted in *Congressional Record,* December 21, 1987, 37084.

14. Representative Jim Cooper (D-TN) quoted in *Congressional Record,* December 21, 1987, 37074.

15. Representative Barbara Vucanovich (R-NV) quoted in *Congressional Quarterly* (1990, 483).

16. Senator Harry Reid (D-NV) quoted in *Congressional Quarterly* (1990, 483).

17. Sen. Johnston quoted in *Congressional Quarterly* (1990, 483).

18. Sen. Reid quoted in *Congressional Record,* December 21, 1987, 37632.

19. Senator George Mitchell (D-ME) quoted in *Congressional Record,* December 21, 1987, 37702.

20. See the comments of Senator Chic Hecht (R-NV) quoted in *Congressional Record,* December 21, 1987, 37690–37691.

21. Representative James Bilbray (D-NV) quoted in *Congressional Record,* December 21, 1987, 37076.

22. Rep. Bilbray quoted in *Congressional Record,* December 21, 1987, 37076.

23. Letter to Representative Kent Hance (D-TX) from Charles H. Murphy, vice-president of government and consumer affairs for Frito-Lay quoted in Carter (1987, 157).

24. Consistent with Kunreuther and Easterling's (1990, 252–56) findings, Nevada has shown no interest in taking on nuclear waste in return for financial compensation and with the state's 2002 veto, compensation appears to be precluded.

25. Various proposals were offered in 1982 by Representative Al Swift (D-WA), Representative Ron Wyden (D-OR) and Representative Stanley Lundine (D-NY), to name a few. In addition, we discussed earlier the proposal of Rep. Udall in 1987 that was rejected in conference.

26. Establishing this point requires only that the reader skim any history of relations between Congress and DOE. Several authors have made this argument, including Jacob (1990) and Carter (1987).

27. The deal discussed earlier on MRS with the Tennessee delegation serves as one prime example.

28. As discussed earlier, because it was a reconciliation bill, the filibuster was not an option for opponents and few wanted to vote down the entire reconciliation bill merely because of the nuclear waste provisions.

29. Sen. Johnston quoted in *Congressional Quarterly* (1990, 483).

30. See, for instance, Madison's argument in Federalist #51 that the public interest will actually be preserved by connecting "the interest of the man with the constitutional right of the place."

Notes to Chapter Four

1. It is true that while legislators no longer seek to protect domestic industries by setting individual tariff rates, they have employed other policy tools to provide relief from foreign competition. Nevertheless, the move from the setting of tariff schedules to what Pietro Nivola (1993) has called "procedural protectionism" is a significant policy change worthy of examination.

2. The law was the Duty Act of July 4, 1789, I Stat. 24.

3. Smoot was defeated in the general election and Hawley failed even to secure his party's nomination.

4. President William J. Clinton quoted in Ifill (1993, A2).

5. The NAFTA implementing legislation was PL 103–182.

6. The Omnibus Trade and Competitiveness Act of 1988 is PL 100–418.

7. See, for instance, the argument presented at a variety of points in Gilligan 1997, 10, 51, 136.

8. President Clinton quoted in Mills (1993, A28).

9. Representative Tom Lewis (R-FL) quoted in Bradsher (1993, A21).

10. Representative Glenn English (D-OK) quoted in *Congressional Quarterly* (1997, 158).

11. Sen. Dole (R-KS), Sen. Mitchell (D-ME), Rep. Foley (D-WA), and Rep. Michel (R-IL) all voted yea in their respective chambers.

12. See Ifill (1993, A2).

13. After many failed attempts by President Clinton and President Bush, the Congress finally granted the president renewed fast-track authority in August 2002. The bill was PL 107–210.

Notes to Chapter Five

1. These figures exclude social insurance taxes and contributions.

2. For a more complete discussion of the lure of tax expenditures versus tax rate reductions, see Arnold (1990, 198–204).

3. For an excellent discussion of the importance and magnitude of tax expenditures as an ignored part of the American welfare state see Howard (1997).

4. Representative Willis Gradison (R-OH) quoted in Birnbaum and Murray (1987, 108).

5. Senator Russell Long (D-LA) quoted in Birnbaum and Murray (1987, 15)

6. See, for instance, Surrey (1981, 185).

7. By "horizontal equity" I mean that one goal of reformers was to ensure that persons who receive similar income pay similar amounts in taxes. Tax expenditures obviously frustrate horizontal equity because they give special tax breaks to individuals or corporations engaged in particular kinds of economic activity without providing a compensating benefit to others. The result is greater variance in tax liability between persons with equal incomes.

8. Arnold also finds the explanation for tax reform offered by Birnbaum and Murray to be deficient. Birnbaum and Murray (1987, 175) argue that the vote on the House floor for TRA86 showed that "under the right conditions, members of Congress would cast a vote for a tax bill that was in the general interest, even though it went against the wishes of powerful lobbyists." But as Arnold (1990, 213, n42) points out, "Birnbaum and Murray never specify what those conditions or circumstances might be."

9. Arnold (1990, 219) points out, "all that the proponents of a specific tax preference had to do to pressure committee members to retain a favorite tax preference was to demand a recorded vote." Indeed, despite the fact that the doors were closed, Strahan (1990, 144) points out that proponents of specific tax breaks were successful in forcing 48 recorded votes in the Ways and Means markup.

10. Representative Dan Rostenkowski (D-IL) quoted in Conlan, Wrightson, and Beam (1990, 115).

11. Representative Thomas P. O'Neill (D-MA) quoted in Birnbaum and Murray (1987, 175).

12. Representative Thomas P. (Tip) O'Neill (D-MA) quoted in Conlan, Wrightson, and Beam (1990, 113).

13. Senator Daniel Patrick Moynihan (D-NY) quoted in Conlan, Wrightson, and Beam (1990, 184).

14. Anonymous administration official quoted in Brownstein (1985, 247).

15. Quoted in Conlan, Wrightson, and Beam (1990, 175).

16. Senator Russell Long (D-LA) quoted in Conlan, Wrightson, and Beam (1990, 176).

17. Representative Dan Rostenkowski (D-IL) quoted in Conlan, Wrightson, and Beam (1990, 93).

18. See Appendices A and B in Birnbaum and Murray (1987) for a detailed graphic on the evolution of major provisions in TRA86.

19. Quoted in Strahan (1990, 150–51).

20. Gina Despres quoted in Conlan, Wrightson, and Beam (1990, 182).

21. This line of argument is similar in a way to the description of legislative behavior in Fiorina (1989). Fiorina argues that legislators profit politically by claiming credit for the creation of big government and then profit politically by becoming the monopoly provider of "bureaucratic unsticking" services to constituents. One could similarly argue that members of Congress profited politically by creating the myriad of tax preferences that they then sought to claim credit for eliminating in 1986. I would not ascribe any conspiratorial or even remotely organized intent to this pattern of policymaking. The only point of relevance here is that the *timing* is important. TRA86 could only have happened after a period of expanding tax preferences like the one in the late 1970s.

22. Quoted in Strahan (1990, 147).

23. This line of argument flies in the face of many of the arguments advanced by observers such as James Sundquist (1988–89). Sundquist complains that political science needs to rescue America's governing institutions from the "electoral accident" of divided government. The main deficiency of divided government, he claims, is immobility—the inability of our governing institutions to act decisively to resolve obvious policy problems. The view advanced by Rostenkowski here implies that divided government may, in fact, be *more capable* of acting decisively.

24. Quoted in Conlan, Wrightson, and Beam (1990, 244).

25. These are Arnold's words substituting for Mayhew's claim that members of Congress are "single-minded seekers of reelection." For a more extensive discussion of the meaning of this distinction, see Arnold (1990, 5–6).

Notes to Chapter Six

1. This question is the subject of a significant and growing literature. Kingdon (1995) remains a classic in this field, but also see Mucciaroni (1995).

2. I borrow this descriptive term from Goren (1998).

3. See, for instance, Theodore Lowi (1979) and Sundquist (1981).

4. This concept is drawn from Kiewiet and McCubbins (1991). For a fuller description of this idea, see their excellent treatment of the problems that attend delegation.

5. The new round was authorized in 2001 in PL 107–107. Some legislators continue to try to derail the scheduled round and have come close. On June 4, 2003, the Senate turned back an amendment that would have canceled the coming round by a vote of 42–53.

6. Underscoring how the moment in political time may have changed, the House vote on the conference report granting fast-track authority (PL 107–210) was a razor-thin 215–212. The Central American Free Trade Agreement that has resulted from this authority is expected to face a very difficult fight in the Congress.

BIBLIOGRAPHY

Ackerman, Bruce, and David Golove. 1995. *Is NAFTA Constitutional?* Cambridge, MA: Harvard University Press.

Advisory Commission on Intergovernmental Relations. 1984. *Significant Features of Fiscal Federalism,* 1984 edition.

Aldrich, John H., and David W. Rohde. 1998. "The Consequences of Party Organization in the House: Theory and Evidence on Conditional Party Government." Paper delivered at the Annual Meeting of the Southern Political Science Association, Atlanta, Georgia, October 29–31.

Armey, Dick. 1988. "Base Maneuvers." *Policy Review* (Winter): 70–75.

Arnold, R. Douglas. 1981a. "Legislators, Bureaucrats, and Locational Decisions." *Public Choice* 37: 107–32.

———. 1981b. "The Local Roots of Domestic Policy." In Thomas E. Mann and Norman J. Ornstein, eds., *The New Congress,* 250–87. Washington, D.C.: American Enterprise Institute for Public Policy.

———. 1990. *The Logic of Congressional Action.* New Haven: Yale University Press.

Baldwin, Robert. 1998. "U.S. Trade Policies: The Role of the Executive Branch." In Alan V. Deardorff and Robert M. Stern, eds., *Constituent Interests and U.S. Trade Policies,* 65–88. Ann Arbor: The University of Michigan Press.

Benenson, Bob. 1990. "Members Hustle to Protect Defense Jobs Back Home." *CQ Weekly* 48 (January 13): 87–90.

Birnbaum, Jeffrey H., and Alan S. Murray. 1987. *Showdown at Gucci Gulch.* New York: Vintage Books.

Bradsher, Keith. 1993. "Clinton's Shopping List for Votes Has Ring of Grocery Buyer's List." *New York Times,* November 17, A21.

Brownstein, Ronald. 1985. "Wagering on Tax Reform." *National Journal,* February 2.

Bryan, Richard H. 1987. "The Politics and Promises of Nuclear Waste Disposal: The View from Nevada." *Environment* 29 (October): 14–17, 32–38.

Buchanan, James M. 1987. "Tax Reform as Political Choice." *Economic Perspectives* 1, no. 1 (Summer): 29–35.

Cain, Bruce, John Ferejohn, and Morris Fiorina. 1987. *The Personal Vote: Constituency Service and Electoral Independence.* Cambridge, MA: Harvard University Press.

Campbell, Colton C. 2002. *Discharging Congress: Government by Commission.* Westport, CT: Praeger.

Carter, Luther J. 1987. *Nuclear Imperatives and Public Trust: Dealing with Radioactive Waste.* Washington, D.C.: Resources for the Future.

Congressional Quarterly. 1985. *Congress and the Nation, Volume VI, 1981–1984.* Washington, D.C.: Congressional Quarterly, Inc.

————. 1989. "Bases: A History of Protection by the System." *1988 CQ Almanac.* Washington, D.C.: Congressional Quarterly, Inc., 441.

————. 1990. *Congress and the Nation, Volume VII, 1985–1988.* Washington, D.C.: Congressional Quarterly, Inc.

————. 1993. *Congress and the Nation, Volume VIII, 1989–1992.* Washington, D.C.: Congressional Quarterly, Inc.

————. 1997. *Congress and the Nation, Volume IX, 1993–1996.* Washington, D.C.: Congressional Quarterly, Inc.

Conlan, Timothy J., Margaret T. Wrightson, and David R. Beam. 1990. *Taxing Choices: The Politics of Tax Reform.* Washington D.C.: CQ Press.

Cook, Charles E. "Base Closing Furor: Minimal Political Impact for Members." *Roll Call,* March 18, 1993.

Cox, Gary W., and Mathew D. McCubbins. 1993. *Legislative Leviathan: Party Government in the House.* Los Angeles: University of California Press.

Deering, Christopher J. 1996. "Congress, the President and Automatic Government: The Case of Military Base Closures." In James Thurber, ed., *Rivals for Power,* 153–69. Washington, D.C.: CQ Press.

Denzau, Arthur T., and Michael C. Munger. "Legislators and Interest Groups: How Unorganized Interests Get Represented." *American Political Science Review* 80 (March 1986): 89–106.

Department of Defense. 1995. *Base Closure and Realignment Report.* March.

Derthick, Martha, and Paul J. Quirk. 1985. *The Politics of Deregulation.* Washington, D.C.: The Brookings Institution.

Destler, I. M. 1998. "Congress, Constituencies, and U.S. Trade Policy." In Deardorff and Stern, eds., *Constituent Interests and U.S. Trade Policies,* 93–108. Ann Arbor: University of Michigan Press.

Dewar, Helen. 1997. "Behind the About-Face on Base Closings." *The Washington Post,* July 16, A17.

Dexter, Lewis Anthony. 1969. "Congressmen and the Making of Military Policy." In Robert L. Peabody and Nelson W. Polsby, eds., *New Perspectives on the House of Representatives.* 2nd ed., 175–94. Chicago: Rand McNally.

Ensign, John. 1998. "Should the House Pass H.R. 1270, the Nuclear Waste Policy Act of 1997?" *Congressional Digest* 77, no. 1 (January): 23, 25, 27, 29.

Fenno, Richard F. 1973. *Congressmen in Committees.* Boston: Little, Brown Publishers.

Fiorina, Morris P. 1989. *Congress: Keystone of the Washington Establishment.* 2nd ed. New Haven, CT: Yale University Press.

General Accounting Office. 1985. "Department of Energy's Initial Efforts to Implement the Nuclear Waste Policy Act of 1982." GAO/RCED 85–27 (January 10).

Gilligan, Michael J. 1997. *Empowering Exporters: Reciprocity, Delegation, and Collective Action in American Trade Policy.* Ann Arbor: The University of Michigan Press.

Goren, Lilly Josephine. 1998. "BRACC to the Future: Evasive Delegation and Blame Avoidance in Base Closings." Ph.D. dissertation, Boston College.

Gross, Neil. 1998. "Between a Rock and a Hot Place. *Business Week,* no. 3574 (April 20): 134.

Hadwiger, David Casimir. 1993. "Military Base Closures: How Congress Balances Geographic and General Interests." Ph.D. dissertation. University of California, Berkeley.

Hager, George, and Eric Pianin. 1996. "Bipartisan Buyers Beware." *The Washington Post National Weekly Edition,* December 2–8, 21–22.

Hansen, Wendy L. 1990. "The International Trade Commission and the Politics of Protectionism." *American Political Science Review* 84, no. 1 (March): 21–46.

Hook, Janet. 1993. "Special NAFTA Report: The Uphill Battle for Votes Produces a Whirl of Wooing and Wheedling." *CQ Weekly* 51 (November 6): 3014.

Howard, Christopher. 1997. *The Hidden Welfare State: Tax Expenditures and Social Policy in the United States.* Princeton, NJ: Princeton University Press.

Idelson, Holly. 1991a. "Nevada Prepares for Battle on Nuclear Waste—Again." *CQ Weekly* 49 (September 7): 2558.

———. 1991b. "Energy: Panel Acts on Waste Dump, But Bill's Future Doubtful." *CQ Weekly* 49 (September 14): 2613.

———. 1992. "High Noon at Yucca Mountain." *CQ Weekly* 50 (October 10): 3142.

Ifill, Gwen. 1993. "Clinton Extends an Unusual Offer to Republicans on Pact." *New York Times,* November 13, A2.

Jacob, Gerald. 1990. *Site Unseen: The Politics of Siting a Nuclear Waste Repository.* Pittsburgh, PA: University of Pittsburgh Press.

Jacobson, Gary C. 2001. *The Politics of Congressional Elections.* 5th ed. New York: Longman.

Joint Committee on Taxation. 1985. *Estimates of Federal Tax Expenditures for Fiscal Years 1986–1990* (JCS-8–85), April 12.

———. 1987. *Estimates of Federal Tax Expenditures for Fiscal Years 1988–1992* (JCS-3–87), February 27.

Kiewiet, D. Roderick, and Mathew D. McCubbins. 1991. *The Logic of Delegation.* Chicago: University of Chicago Press.

Kingdon, John W. 1989. *Congressmen's Voting Decisions.* 3rd ed. Ann Arbor: The University of Michigan Press.

———. 1995. *Agendas, Alternatives, and Public Policies.* 2nd ed. New York: HarperCollins.

Kitfield, James. 1997. "Cohen Opts for the Middle Ground." *National Journal,* May 24, 1042.

Korn, Jessica. 1996. *The Power of Separation.* Princeton, NJ: Princeton University Press.

Krehbiel, Keith. 1991. *Information and Legislative Organization.* Ann Arbor: The University of Michigan Press.

Kunreuther, Howard, and Douglas Easterling. 1990. "Are Risk-Benefit Tradeoffs Possible in Siting Hazardous Facilities?" *The American Economic Review* 80, no. 2 (May): 252–56.

League of Women Voters Education Fund. 1993. *The Nuclear Waste Primer,* 1993. Rev. ed. Washington, D.C.: The League of Women Voters Education Fund.

Lindsay, James M. 1990. "Parochialism, Policy, and Constituency Constraints: Congressional Voting on Strategic Weapons Systems." *American Journal of Political Science* 34, no. 4 (November): 936–60.

Lowi, Theodore. 1979. *The End of Liberalism.* 2nd ed. New York: Norton.

Mansbridge, Jane J. 1990. *Beyond Self-Interest.* Chicago: University of Chicago Press.

Markey, Edward. 1998. "Should the House Pass H.R. 1270, the Nuclear Waste Policy Act of 1997?" *Congressional Digest* 77, no. 1 (January): 15, 17, 19.

Mayer, Kenneth R. 1995. "Closing Military Bases (Finally): Solving Collective Dilemmas through Delegation." *Legislative Studies Quarterly* 20, no. 3 (August): 393–413.

Mayhew, David R. 1974. *Congress: The Electoral Connection.* New Haven: Yale University Press.

McCutcheon, Chuck. 1998. "Nevada Waste Site Defeated in Election-Year Tussle over Reid's Senate Seat." *CQ Weekly* 56 (June 6): 1536.

McKeown, Timothy J. 1994. "What Forces Shape American Trade Policy?" In Charles F. Doran and Gregory P. Marchildon, eds., *The NAFTA Puzzle: Political Parties and Trade in North America,* 65–86. San Francisco: Westview Press.

Mills, Joshua. 1993. "Business Lobbying for Trade Pact Appears to Sway Few in Congress." *New York Times,* November 13, A28.

Mills, Mike. 1988. "Base Closings: The Political Pain Is Limited." *CQ Weekly* 46 (December 31): 3629.

———. 1989. "A Dogged, if Futile, Trench War Is Planned by Some on Hill." *CQ Weekly* 47 (March 25): 660–62.

Morrison, David C. 1989. "Caught Off Base." *National Journal,* April 1, 801.

Mucciaroni, Gary. 1995. *Reversals of Fortune: Public Policy and Private Interests.* Washington, D.C.: The Brookings Institution.

Nivola, Pietro S. 1993. *Regulating Unfair Trade.* Washington, D.C.: The Brookings Insitution.

O'Halloran, Sharyn. 1994. *Politics, Process, and American Trade Policy.* Ann Arbor: The University of Michigan Press.

Palmer, Elizabeth A. 1991. "Commission May Help Ease Members' Unsavory Task." *CQ Weekly* 49 (March 2): 555. .

———. 1994. "Former Sen. Dixon to Oversee Painful New Round of Cuts." *CQ Weekly* 52 (October 8): 2898.

Richter, Paul. 1997. "Senate Rejects Bid for More Base Closures." *Los Angeles Times,* July 10, A19.

Rohde, David W. 1994. "Parties and Committees in the House: Member Motivations, Issues, and Institutional Arrangements." *Legislative Studies Quarterly* 19, no. 3 (August): 341–59.

Rourke, Francis E., and Paul R. Schulman. 1989. "Adhocracy in Policy Development." *The Social Science Journal* 26, no. 2 (April): 131–42.

Sandford, Cedric. 1993. *Successful Tax Reform*. Trowbridge, England: Fiscal Publications.

Schafer, Susanne M. 1998. "Cohen to Seek New Base Closures." *Associated Press*, April 2.

Shepsle, Kenneth A. 1989. "The Changing Textbook Congress." In John E. Chubb and Paul E. Peterson, eds., *Can the Government Govern?*, 238–66. Washington, D.C.: The Brookings Institution.

Sinclair, Barbara. 2000. *Unorthodox Lawmaking: New Legislative Processes in the U.S. Congress*. 2nd ed. Washington, D.C.: Congressional Quarterly Press.

Skowronek, Stephen. 2003. "Presidential Leadership in Political Time." In Michael Nelson, ed., *The Presidency and the Political System*. 7th ed., 111–57. Washington, D.C.: Congressional Quarterly Press.

Snyder, , James M., Jr. 1993. "Comment on 'Local Interests, Central Leadership, and the Passage of TRA86.'" *Journal of Policy Analysis and Management*. 12, no. 1: 181–88.

Strahan, Randall. 1990. *New Ways and Means*. Chapel Hill: The University of North Carolina Press.

Sundquist, James. 1981. *The Decline and Resurgence of Congress*. Washington, D.C.: The Brookings Institution.

———. 1988–89. "Needed: A Political Theory for the New Era of Coalition Government in the United States." *Political Science Quarterly* 103, no. 4 (Winter): 613–35.

Surrey, Stanley S. 1981. "Our Troubled Tax Policy: False Routes and Proper Paths to Change." *Tax Notes*, February 2.

Tax Foundation. 1988. *Facts and Figures on Government Finance*. 23rd ed. Baltimore, MD: The Johns Hopkins University Press, Table 31.

———. 1991. *Facts and Figures on Government Finance*. 26th ed. Baltimore, MD: The Johns Hopkins University Press, Table 31.

Twight, Charlotte. 1990. "Department of Defense Attempts to Close Military Bases: The Political Economy of Congressional Resistance." In Robert Higgs, ed., *Arms, Politics and the Economy*, 237–80. New York: Holmes & Meier,

Vick, Karl. 1995. "It's Closing Time for Base Commission." *The Washington Post*, December 29, A21.

Weaver, R. Kent. 1986. "The Politics of Blame Avoidance." *Journal of Public Policy* 6, no. 4: 371–98.

Weingast, Barry R., and William J. Marshall. 1988. "The Industrial Organization of Congress; Or, Why Legislatures, Like Firms, Are Not Organized as Markets." *Journal of Political Economy* 96, no. 1: 132–63.

Wiarda, Howard J. 1994. "The U.S. Domestic Politics of the U.S.–Mexico Free Trade Agreement." In M. Delal Baer and Sidney Weintraub, eds., *The NAFTA Debate: Grappling with Unconventional Trade Issues*, 117–44. Boulder, CO: Lynne Rienner Publishers, Inc.,

Witte, John F. 1985. *The Politics and the Development of the Federal Income Tax*. Madison, WI: The University of Wisconsin Press.

INDEX

PARLIAMENTS AND LEGISLATURES
Janet M. Box-Steffensmeier and David T. Canon, Series Editors

www.ingramcontent.com/pod-product-compliance
Lightning Source LLC
Chambersburg PA
CBHW020705270326
41928CB00005B/281